CSI

CONCEPTS · SOURCES · INTEGRATION

A STEP-BY-STEP GUIDE
TO WRITING YOUR LITERATURE REVIEW
IN COMMUNICATION STUDIES

REBECCA M.L. CURNALIA · AMBER L. FERRIS

Youngstown State
University

University of Akron
Wayne College

Kendall Hunt
publishing company

www.kendallhunt.com
Send all inquiries to:
4050 Westmark Drive
Dubuque, IA 52004-1840

Copyright © 2014 by Kendall Hunt Publishing Company

ISBN 978-1-4652-5056-8

Printed in the United States of America

Contents

Preface

Welcome to *Concepts, Sources, Integration* (*CSI*). *CSI* is both a "how-to" guide to help students prepare research papers in communication studies and also an introduction to the mindset and orientation we all need as communication scholars: we should be inquisitive investigators. We are mixed methodologists with diverse research interests that cut-across multiple areas of study in communication and several academic disciplines, so we wanted to present an inclusive, flexible guide to help you appreciate and capitalize on the rich diversity in communication studies. Of course, the very thing that makes us unique, flexible, and dynamic as a discipline – our diversity – also presents challenges for us as researchers. We have to be able to find, read, and think critically about research from different theoretical and methodological perspectives, write for a broad audience, and disseminate our research through numerous channels to share our knowledge. *CSI* is a starting point for communication students to begin reading, writing, and researching in the discipline and a guide that you can refer back to for many types of writing assignments in the future. We hope that it also introduces you to new ways of thinking about and using information regardless of whether you are writing a term paper for an undergraduate course, a thesis, or a blog post.

About the Authors

Rebecca M. L. Curnalia, Ph.D.

Dr. Curnalia is an Associate Professor in the Department of Communication at Youngstown State University. Her background is in media and persuasion theory, which she applies to research politics. You can read Dr. Curnalia's research in *Communication Research Reports, Qualitative Research Reports in Communication, The American Communication Journal*, and in recently published books such as *Venomous Speech: Problems with American Political Discourse on the Right and Left* and *Reality TV: Oddities of Culture*. Dr. Curnalia is also the lead author of *Becoming a Critic: An Introduction to Analyzing Media Content*. In addition to research in media and politics, Dr. Curnalia also  actively engages in the scholarship of teaching and learning by teaching short courses and presenting best practices for assessment at regional and national conferences, leading assessment efforts in YSU's communication program, working on university-wide assessment of student learning, and participating in the National Communication Association's Learning Outcomes Project.

Dedication

For the many amazing women who have mentored me as a writer. Beginning with my mother, who worked with me on my book reports, to Joanne Williams at Olivet College who taught my journalism courses, to Mary Lynn Henningsen at Northern Illinois University who encouraged me to internalize APA, to Nichole Egbert at Kent State who taught me how to teach writing. Each of you has had a profound effect on me as a scholar and instructor.

Thank you.

Amber L. Ferris, Ph.D.

Dr. Ferris is an Assistant Professor of Communication at The University of Akron Wayne College. She enjoys studying the effects of television on viewers, as well as the impact of new media use, including social networks and mobile phones. Her research has been published in the *Journal of Communication, Computers in Human Behavior,* and the *Ohio Communication Journal* as well as in edited books on mobile phone use, the political climate after 9/11, and prosocial behavior on television. Dr. Ferris currently serves as the assistant editor for the *Ohio Communication Journal.* She has also reviewed manuscripts for the *Journal of Communication, Journal of Broadcasting & Electronic Media, Journal of Personal and Social Relationships, The Howard Journal of Communications* and the *British Journal of Education, Society, & Behavioural Science.*

Dedication

For my partner, Tabitha, who consistently tolerates life with an academic. Thank you for supporting me through the long days and nights of writing.

I love you.

Introduction

WHY DO I HAVE TO DO THIS?
THE VALUE OF ACADEMIC RESEARCH
AND WRITING SKILLS

Welcome to *CSI: A Step-by-Step Guide to Writing Your Literature Review in Communication Studies*! After years of teaching students how to write their first literature reviews, we decided that there was a need for a textbook that took students step-by-step through the process of conceptualizing, reading research, and writing in Communication Studies. As an interdisciplinary field, students in communication programs have a unique opportunity to draw on academic literature from a broad range of social sciences and humanities fields to answer practical questions about human communication processes and effects. But this presents a unique challenge too.

As an interdisciplinary field with diverse theories, concepts, methods, and bodies of literature, it can be particularly difficult to decide what to research and where to look to find sources for our papers. Further, once we have sources, they often present research from different philosophical, theoretical, and methodological approaches, which can make synthesizing and reaching conclusions particularly challenging, even for seasoned and experienced researchers. Further, when we write, we have to write for the broad and diverse audience of communication scholars and practitioners.

We liken this process to being a detective, and we use the CSI theme to frame our discussion of the steps involved in conceptualizing, planning, researching, and writing your first literature review. Ultimately, like being a detective, successfully answering your research question involves an inquisitive, open, and critical mind. Indeed, this book is as much about your orientation toward finding and interpreting information as it is a "how-to" guide to writing literature reviews. A good researcher, much like a good detective, asks questions, looks in different places to find answers, and finds trends in the evidence that point to conclusions; they are careful, aware, and inquisitive. This orientation toward information is one that you can apply to answer many of the questions you face in life, from deciding about medical care, to buying a car or a house, to making decisions about how to raise children. The ability to find, analyze, and apply information from different sources will help you reach well-reasoned decisions.

So, this inquisitive, open-minded approach to finding answers extends beyond academic pursuits and the classroom. We sincerely hope that the research and writing skills you learn in this book also translate to practical, real-life information literacy and writing skills that will serve you throughout your careers and in your own social lives. The ability to find, interpret, and reach conclusions is an important life skill in the digital information age and one that we, as your professors and mentors, hope to see you use throughout your lives. Our belief in research as a necessary and practical skill stems from the findings of the Boyer Commission.

The Importance of Researching Skills in the Digital Information Age

In 1998 the Boyer Commission, funded by the Carnegie Foundation, made a series of recommendations about how to improve education at research universities. One of their key findings was that, beginning early in the undergraduate curriculum, students should be participating in research. In fact, they argued, "Undergraduates need to become an active part of the audience for research" and learn how to read, write about, and conduct research because "the abilities to identify, analyze, and resolve problems will prove invaluable in professional life and in citizenship" (p. 17). The commission argued that outdated methods of educating, which relied on lectures and exams, did little to create productive, critically thinking, problem-solving graduates. Higher education, they argued, was not preparing students for the fast-changing information environment.

Indeed, the memorization of facts may be less essential to your long-term professional and personal success compared to learning how to access, evaluate, synthesize, and reach conclusions based on solid evidence. Anyone can find factual information by simply going to Google. So now in the digital information age, the emphasis needs to shift to developing students' information literacy rather than information retention.

Unfortunately, research suggests that recent college graduates think that they are good at finding and synthesizing evidence to reach conclusions; however, employers disagree (Grasgreen, 2013). Though the vast majority of grads felt that they had the writing skills that employers were looking for, less than half of employers agreed that graduates were able to write "to communicate ideas or explain information clearly" (para. 5). Further, only 37% of employers agreed that recent graduates were able to make "a decision without having all the facts" (para. 6), and showed concern that students were unable to organize and prioritize. Interestingly, these are all skills related to collecting, critiquing, interpreting, organizing, and writing, which is exactly what we do when we conduct research.

We see a renewed emphasis on undergraduate research throughout research universities in addition to an increased emphasis on writing and oral communication skills (Katkin, 2003). These efforts increasingly take the form of written capstone projects and formal presentations of undergraduate student research. In terms of students in Communication programs, projects such as writing a thesis or an applied research project, presenting it, and also creating a professional portfolio are considered essential final steps toward degree completion (Moore, 1994).

The outcomes associated with the integration of collaborative student research have been promising. Research has suggested that the faculty-student relationship is strengthened by participation in collaborative student research projects

(Rodrick & Dickmeyer, 2002). Students who complete these kinds of projects tend to learn and think in new, complex ways; they appreciate their discipline more, have improved analytical thinking skills, and have the resources to be lifelong learners. Students tend to be resistant to courses that teach research methods and academic writing, but the benefits of these courses far outweigh the challenges.

Relevant Boyer Commission Findings:

- Undergraduates should be actively engaged in the process of academic research, particularly reading and writing about academic research.
- Faculty should be mentors to student-researchers; therefore, learning should be collaborative.
- Written and oral communication skills should be developed throughout the undergraduate degree and culminate in a capstone project.
- Students should learn to write and present information in a way that is accessible to non-academic audiences.

Read the full report here: http://www.niu.edu/engagedlearning/ research/pdfs/Boyer_Report.pdf

Learning Objectives for this Text

Information Literacy

We live in a society that inundates us with information. From 24-hour news cycles to the millions of "hits" we get on Google, we are in an age where information abounds, and our ability to sift through that mountain of information, assess its quality, and draw reasoned conclusions are necessary skills. Therefore, our first objective for this book is to help you become a literate information consumer: to understand how to read, interpret, and evaluate information.

Critical Thinking

The ability to synthesize, compare and contrast, and draw sound conclusions is an essential life skill. Participating in undergraduate research projects increases critical thinking skills (Denny, 2012). Throughout your life, you will have to make many decisions about what to buy, who to vote for, what you should and should not do. The ability to recognize trends and reach reasoned conclusions using sound evidence will be essential to your ability to make important life decisions. Thus, our second objective for students using this text is to learn how to think about information sources, content, and trends critically.

Problem-Solving

Knowing how to ask pointed questions and find answers is an essential personal and professional skill, particularly in our information-saturated world.

Simply going to Google and skimming the first few dozen hits from a topic search is not sufficient. Much of what we know about society, culture, and individuals is the result of research. Therefore, being able to find, read, analyze, and synthesize research findings will help you answer questions and solve problems that come up in your everyday personal and professional life. Participating in research is beneficial to students because it increases students' ability to be independent learners (Ishiyama, 2002). Research is a problem-solving process. We begin with a question centered on some real-life problem. We have to use troubleshooting skills when finding too many or too few sources. We then try to reach conclusions when the information we find is sometimes incomplete or inconclusive. Therefore, our third objective for students using this book is to develop problem-solving skills that will help them navigate the rich information environment we live in today.

Writing

We hope that students will grow as writers over the course of this text. Though we cannot possibly teach you everything you need to know about writing in one brief guide, one of our primary objectives is to point out some of the most common issues that arise as students begin to write literature reviews. Beyond academic writing, our communication is increasingly text-based. Text messages and emails are replacing phone calls and meetings. Even classes are moving from face-to-face instruction to online instruction, leaving the majority of instruction to written explanations, grades, and written comments on projects. Therefore, writing skills are that much more essential to your personal and professional success than they were just 20 years ago. Students who were involved in research during their undergraduate degrees report being better writers and communicators after graduation (Bauer & Bennett, 2003). We do this by going over, in some detail, strategies for organizing ideas and communicating ideas clearly, concisely, and correctly.

Ethics

"Ethics is what you do when nobody's looking" (Wright, 1989, p. A7). Being honest and ethical is crucial, not only in an academic setting, but in your professional and personal lives. The National Communication Association's Credo for Ethical Communication states that the values of "truthfulness, accuracy, honesty, and reason [are] essential to the integrity of communication" (NCA, 1999, para. 2). Chances are you have been learning these values throughout your life, and you will continue to develop your sense of ethics in your education and beyond. The skills that you will learn throughout this text will help you act in an ethical manner, including how to synthesize and paraphrase properly, as well as how to credit your sources and cite properly.

You can access NCA's full Credo for Ethical Communication at: http://www.natcom.org/Tertiary.aspx?id=2119

Introduction to the 8 Steps

In the following chapters, we introduce you to the steps involved in researching and writing for your first literature review. Each chapter in this text is a step toward completing a well focused, researched, organized, and written literature review. Your goals should be to find the best sources in order to find similarities, differences, and ambiguities regarding a topic. You will then use that information to synthesize and develop a clear and rational argument for a series of conclusions (hypotheses) and areas of future research needed (research questions) about how specific concepts are related to each other.

The 8 steps overviewed in this guide are:

1. Narrowing your topic and formulating a problem question
2. Searching for sources
3. Reading and taking notes on sources
4. Synthesizing sources
5. Writing an outline of the evidence
6. Writing a review of the evidence
7. Editing your review
8. Presenting your review

Lastly, we discuss uses for your completed literature review.

The first step is to develop your research focus. You need to take inventory of what you are interested in then look at relevant subtopics to narrow the focus of your paper. Then you formulate a problem question, which will guide what concepts or theories you will focus on in your paper. Once you have settled on a specific set of concepts, you then thoroughly search through the existing academic literature to find articles that study those variables and assess how those variables are studied, how they may be related to each other, and what research remains to be done on those variables. Finally, using the notes taken on the articles most relevant to your paper's purpose, you put together a paper that organizes the evidence and compares, contrasts, and critiques their methods and results to justify the hypotheses proposed at the end of the paper.

There are several different types of literature reviews. Some are historical, and trace how a theory, concept, or line of research has developed over time. Some literature reviews develop a new theory or model to explain human communication processes and outcomes. Literature reviews may be summaries of existing research on a theory, or they may be critiques that point out areas of research that are flawed, unclear, or require further development. The type of paper you write depends in the nature of the project you are assigned to complete and what you find when you are looking through the academic evidence about your topic.

There are journals in communication studies that are devoted entirely to publishing literature reviews, such as *Communication Theory* and *Communication Yearbook*. For solid examples of literature reviews, see either of these highly regarded publications from the International Communication Association or a chapter in any of their *Handbook* series: http://www.icahdq.org/pubs/other.asp

REFERENCES

Bauer, K. W., & Bennett, J. S. (2003). Alumni perceptions used to assess undergraduate research experience. *Journal of Higher Education, 74*, 210–230.

Boyer Commission on Educating Undergraduates in the Research University. (1998). Reinventing undergraduate education: A blueprint for America's research universities. Stony Brook, NY: State University of New York-Stony Brook.

Denny, J. P. (2012). The relationship between undergraduate research and critical thinking skills. Unpublished Doctoral Dissertation. Gainesville, FL: University of Florida.

Grasgreen, A. (2013). Qualified in their own minds: More data show students unprepared for work, but what to do about it? *Inside Higher Ed*. Retrieved from http://www.insidehighered.com/news/2013/10/29/more-data-show-students-unprepared-work-what-do-about-it

Ishiyama, I. (2002). Does early participation in undergraduate students benefit social science and humanities students? *Journal of College Students, 36*(3), 380–386.

Katkin, W. (2003). The Boyer Commission report and its impact on undergraduate research. *New Directions for Teaching and Learning, 93*, 19–38.

Moore, R. C. (1994). The capstone course. In W. G. Christ (Ed.) *Assessing communication education: A handbook for media, speech & theatre educators* (pp. 155–179). Washington, DC: National Communication Association.

National Communication Association. (1999). Credo for ethical communication. Retrieved from http://www.natcom.org/Tertiary.aspx?id=2119.

Rodrick, R., & Dickmeyer, L. (2002). Providing undergraduate research opportunities for communication students: A curricular approach. *Communication Education, 51*, 40–50.

Wright, J. (1989, June 15). Real ethics: What you do when nobody's looking. *The Beaver County Times*, A7. Retrieved from http://news.google.com/newspapers?nid=2004&dat=19890614&id=V7oiAAAAIBAJ&sjid=SLUFAAAAIBAJ&pg=2808,2709037

STEP 1

The First Step in Your Investigation: Decide What You're Looking For

The most difficult part of many investigations is deciding where to start. Often, detectives on *CSI* follow a familiar pattern in their investigations, trying to figure out the "who, what, when, where, why" of a crime. These are the same types of things we consider when deciding on a topic to research in communication: Who are we interested in studying? What do people do in different situations? When do people and relationships change? Where are certain types of communication expected and appropriate? Why do people communicate and react the way they do? To try to focus your attention, we will cover some of the specific who, what, when, where, and why questions we pose in different communication contexts.

Investigators also often develop a "theory" about the crime, then collect evidence and allow their theory to change as they find new clues. If a detective sets out in an investigation with a predetermined conclusion, then chances are he or she will miss essential evidence, and maybe waste time and resources pursuing the wrong leads. The key to a quality investigation is to keep an open mind. We may have a hunch about our topic (e.g., I may think that Computer Mediated Communication (CMC) is damaging our interpersonal relationships), but I have to keep an open mind, look at the evidence, and be willing to accept the fact that I may be entirely wrong. Therefore, we begin our investigation with a *question*.

THIS CHAPTER COVERS:

A. Research Within a Communication Context
B. Choose Concepts and Variables Within the Context that is of Interest to You
   1. Concepts and Variables in Communication
   2. Understanding the Jargon: Know What Your Variables are Called in the Communication Literature
   3. Determine if There is a Theory that Can Help You Focus Your Topic
C. Pose an Interesting, Important Question
   1. Types of Questions: Fact, Value, and Policy
D. Define Target Variables:
   1. Independent and Dependent Variables
   2. Reportative, Stipulative, and Operational Definitions

Chinese philosopher Lao-Tsu observed, "a journey of a thousand miles begins with a single step." When you are assigned a literature review for the first time, the task can seem as insurmountable as a thousand-mile hike. But if we take it step-by-step, while keeping in mind the big picture and our end goal, writing your first literature review will not feel so daunting.

Choosing a topic for your paper, if one is not assigned to you, is the first step toward completing a literature review. This can be particularly difficult because the field of communication is very broad and includes research in many different contexts. Chances are, if you've been studying communication for a few years, there are also many topics that are intriguing to you across the different communication contexts.

Though the variables explored in each context are similar, how they are defined and applied in academic research may be very different from one context to the next. So, the first step to choosing a topic is to select a general context about which you are interested in reading and writing. Then, you consider the specific communication variables within that context that are of interest to you. Next, you look at the existing academic research to see what theories or areas of research you should focus on that incorporate your variables of interest.

A. Research Within a Communication Context

The first thing to do is decide on a topic that is appropriate to your theory, professional, and/or personal interests. The context in which you do your research should be related to the context of the coursework you've focused on in communication studies and/or your personal interests, professional interests, or academic goals (like going to graduate school). What you choose to research should be something particularly interesting to you personally. The more interested you are in your topic, the easier it will be to work on it over the course of a semester. Interpersonal, organizational, persuasion, intercultural, gender, political, media, new media, group, public/rhetorical, and health communication are popular contexts for communication research.

If you're having trouble choosing a general communication context or division of study in Communication, check out the National Communication Association's list of divisions for some ideas about the types of topics that communication scholars research:

http://www.natcom.org/interestgroups/

Scan this QR Code to see NCA's list of interest groups.

Table 1.1 Brief Overview of the Popular Communication Contexts and Examples of What is Studied in Each Context:

Interpersonal	Group	Organization	Traditional Media	New Media/CMC	Politics	Intercultural/Gender	Persuasion	Health
Families/Blended Families	Conflict	Organizational Cultures	Media Depictions	Social Networks	Political News	Culture and Gender Types	Speech/Ad Analysis	PSAs and Health Campaigns
Dating/Marriage/Friendships	Decision-Making	Managerial Communication	Video Games	Websites	Campaign Ads	Communication between Cultures/Gender	Attitude Development and Change	Doctor – Patient Comm
Divorce	Leadership	Employee Satisfaction	TV Effects	Uses of Cell Phones	Political Speeches	Depictions of Gender/Culture	Advertising	Bereavement
Long Distance Relationships	Roles	Corporate Mergers	Media Law/Freedom of Speech	Dating Online	Partisanship	Enculturation/Acculturation/Socialization	Social Influence/Compliance Gaining	Caregiving
Social Networks	Social Groups	PR/Crisis Communication	Cultural Studies	Online Group Processes	Political Discussion	Culture/Gender and Communication Style	Information Processing	Health Education
Maintenance/Conflict	Influence	Coworker Relationships	Media Economics	User Generated Content	Political Activity/Voting	Culture/Gender and Conflict	Message, Source, and Sender Variables	Social Support
Instructional Communication	Cohesion	Networks	Media Genres	Online instruction	Political Parties	Gender Roles	Argument Strength/Quality	Fear Appeals

Clues for Success

Think About Your Experiences to Brainstorm Topics:

© doomu, 2014. Shutterstock, Inc.

- A relationship that you've had or have that you would like to understand better.

- A professional experience you've had that was particularly great or awful.

- A group experience that you've had that went really well or blew up in your face.

- Something about yourself that you would like to understand better.

- The media you enjoy or really dislike.

- Something you find peculiar or intriguing about others that you'd like to explain.

There is a fun and informative interactive tool available through the University of Portland that allows you to click on an area of study, explore specific areas of study in each context, and points you toward relevant publications related to each area of research: http://library2.up.edu/cstnodemap.html. If you have a context in mind, but need help focusing your attention, a tool like this can be very useful.

University of Portland interactive tool

Within the general communication context, there are a lot of different concepts and variables that you could choose to study. For example, in interpersonal, you may look at the concepts of families, dating relationships, sibling relationships, marriages, divorces, blended families, inter-cultural interactions, friendships, social support, or bereavement. Within media, there are new media like computer-mediated communication (CMC), social media, blogs, television, radio, advertising, news, entertainment media, cell phones, and other forms of media technology and content.

Notice, too, that many of these specific areas of research overlap. For example, in new media/CMC you may be interested in online dating, which is also a relevant topic to interpersonal communication scholars. If you have diverse interests in communication studies, there are many ways in which these general contexts of study overlap. If you are interested in both interpersonal communication and mass communication, for example, consider specific areas of study that blend these two areas. You could look at the interpersonal uses of television, such as parasocial relationships. You could look at conversational expectations and media selection. You could even look at TV coviewing as a relationship maintenance strategy.

It will be easier to proceed with your research if you decide at the outset what communication context(s) you are interested in studying, then choose a specific area of study within that or those context(s). This will narrow your literature search and help you focus your paper.

Once you've settled on a context and specific area of research, you should start researching with confidence that your topic and purpose can be developed sufficiently to complete the project but, also, that the topic is narrow enough to cover in a literature review. Therefore, the start of the project entails specifying which concepts you are interested in and what kind of information is available on those concepts.

B. Choose Concepts and Variables Within the Context that is of Interest to You

A **communication variable** is anything related to communication processes and/or effects that varies from person to person or situation to situation. Variables are related to specific concepts and are usually explained as constructs in the academic literature. A **concept** is an abstract idea that represents something concrete (Kerlinger & Lee, 2000). For example, *love* is a concept. It has different meanings to different people and is felt and expressed in many ways. Because there are different types of love, researchers have developed the construct *love styles* (e.g., Lee, 1973). Love styles are a **construct** because researchers have "invented them" for "a specific scientific purpose" (Kerlinger & Lee, p. 40). Concepts and constructs are called **variables** when they are measured in scientific research. So, there is a love styles scale (e.g., Hendrick, Hendrick, & Dicke, 1998) that is used to assess people's ways of experiencing love, and therefore love style is a specific variable.

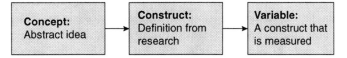

Figure 1.1   Concept-Construct-Variable

1. Concepts and Variables in Communication

What communication concepts are interesting to you and relevant to the context you chose to study? When considering which concepts you're interested in studying, Lasswell's quote about communication studies overviews what we should consider: "*Who* says *what*, to *whom*, in what *channel*, to what *effect*?"

Using his breakdown of the elements of communication, we can look at concepts related to messages, individual senders or receivers, channels, and/or effects.

Who? Individual differences. Personality traits, communication tactics, skills, habits, gender, ethnicity, culture, goals, motives, professional titles, personal experience, relationship status, education, and socioeconomic status are all common examples of variables because they vary from person to person. Also, each of these variables influences how a person communicates in different contexts. In media, we may consider other sender issues, like corporate ownership. When thinking about individual-level variables, consider what it is that makes you who you are: You are a combination of many different experiences, traits, and circumstances. Every one of these things that comprise who you are is an individual-level variable that you may be interested in researching.

Says what? Message content and strategies. Message construction, organization, strategies, visual content, nonverbal elements, and types of appeals are all fodder for research in each of the contexts studied in communication. In interpersonal communication, we look at concepts such as supportive messages, disclosure, openness, conflict styles and management, and immediacy. In group communication, we look at types of leadership, member communication styles, influence in groups, consensus building messages, etc. In mass communication, we look at visual media content, production elements, the values depicted in media content, the behaviors of media characters like violence, aggression, and even consumerism. In persuasion we look at the effects of different types of persuasive appeals, like using fear, citing sources, message order effects, identification, sequential request strategies, and developing strong arguments. These are all message variables that you may be interested in exploring.

To whom? Receiver differences. Receiver variables are also important, and research often looks at how messages are received. The same individual variables that affect how people formulate messages can also affect how messages are received, interpreted, and recalled. We explore variables like attention, information processing, learning, perception, selectivity, cognitive schema, emotional/affective responses, and recall of messages in all communication contexts. These receiver processes are specific variables, often related to individual and situational variables, which determine the effects and effectiveness of messages.

In what channel? There are many channels available to deliver messages, and the number and types of channels available are rapidly increasing. For example, in our interpersonal, group, and organizational relationships we can talk face to face, text, IM, link up on social networks, email, send a letter/memo, etc.

Similarly, in terms of entertainment media, we can watch TV, watch user-generated content online or streaming video online, access content via apps on our phones, and so on. These different channels of delivery affect how messages are received.

With what effect? There are many outcomes of communication worth researching. We often look at attitude change, behavior change, perceptual change, socialization, self perception, ideology, values, satisfaction, liking, involvement, closeness, and even termination in communication research. Each context that we study looks at the effects of different individual variables on the part of the sender and/or receiver, message content, and channel use to determine the effects, or outcomes, of communication. In general, communication researchers are interested in what works, what doesn't, and why, so that we can make recommendations that improve or explain the effects of different types of messages on different people and why people communicate the way they do.

Not all topics require that we research variables or concepts from each of these areas. Rather, we will typically choose a couple of concepts or specific variables related to one or two of these categories. So, thinking about the context that you are researching in, what types of variables are most interesting to you: sender, receiver, content, or channel? What communication outcomes do you think may be related to those variables?

2. Understanding the Jargon: Know What Your Variables are Called in the Communication Literature

Once we have selected a context for our research and identified a couple of concepts we want to research related to the "Who, what, whom, channel, and effect," we need to find out how these concepts are discussed in the communication literature. We often "name" concepts when we turn them into academic constructs, or communication variables. Therefore, we discuss concepts and constructs in a particular way in the literature, so you will need to know what your concepts are called in the academic research before you start looking for resources.

Table 1.2   Examples of "Lay" Concepts and Corresponding Communication
Variables:

Common "Lay" Concepts	Corresponding Communication Constructs and Variables
Breaking-up	Termination, dissolution, divorce
Emotions and feelings	Affect
Reasons we do things	Motives, gratifications, motivation
Relationship happiness and closeness	Satisfaction, positive affect, commitment, intimacy
Liking someone	Attraction, social/physical attraction, reward valence
Hooking up	Attraction, relationship stages (initiation), friends with benefits
Feeling "good" or "bad" about something	Attitude, valence, appraisal
Thinking	Cognition, information processing, elaboration
Weddings	Marriage
Fighting with someone	Conflict, conflict management, negotiation
Speeches	Rhetoric, discourse
Changing minds	Attitude change, perceptions, beliefs, values; persuasion, social influence
Leaving people out	Silencing, muting, symbolic annihilation
Talking	Discourse, dialogue, disclosure, speech acts, verbal messages
Body language	Nonverbal
Race	Ethnicity, culture
Class	Socioeconomic status
Boss	Leader, manager, supervisor
Similarity or being alike	Homophily, identification
Traits	Personality, demographics
Teaching	Instructional communication
Men and women	Gender, biological sex, masculinity/femininity

For example, a lot of students are interested in romantic relationships as their specific context, and are curious about why some relationships work out while others don't. Therefore, they're interested in outcome variables like relationship satisfaction and termination. One thing that can be tricky when you're first immersing yourself in the academic literature is that academic researchers have very specific names for constructs and variables. We also have different definitions of concepts that we use to construct and operationalize variables. So, what we may informally talk about as "being happy" in a relationship is, in the academic literature, called "relationship satisfaction." What we casually call "emotional reactions" researchers often refer to as "affective responses." So, you must learn the correct variable names before beginning to find articles for your study.

Therefore, a good first step toward narrowing your topic is doing some cursory searches of the literature to see what variables are covered in the research related to your topic and what those variables are called. Say for example that we are interested in politics. More specifically, we are interested in knowing *why* we are interested in politics, but others are not. So, we may want to do some research on interest in politics. If we look around in the literature a little bit, we see that "interest" is not often discussed, but political involvement, engagement, and activity are researched extensively. Further, there is research available on involvement and activity in terms of traditional news use, voting, demographics, and social media. Any one of these foci could help us understand why some people aren't interested in politics, and maybe give us insight into how we might get students more interested.

3. Determine if There is a Theory that Can Help You Focus Your Topic

Sometimes there is a theory related to our research interest that will direct our attention toward specific communication concepts we can research. A theory is a statement "about the relationships among abstract concepts or variables" (Hocking et al., 2002, p. 29). Communication theories include clear definitions of concepts, explanations of how those concepts are related to each other, and specific predictions about communication outcomes. Therefore, determining if there is a theory that might guide your research and writing can be extremely useful as the theory will specify the types of concepts and specific variables you should look at and will serve as an organizing principle when considering how those variables are related to each other.

Here is a chart that overviews some of the more common theories in communication studies. Do any of them sound interesting to you?

Table 1.3 Common Communication Studies Theories

Interpersonal	Group/Organizational	Mass/New Media	Intercultural/Gender	Persuasion/Rhetoric/PR
Action Assembly Theory (use of memory to form messages)	Adaptive Structuration Theory (use of rules and resources to form systems)	Agenda Setting Theory (how news media tell us what's important)	Anxiety-Uncertainty Management Theory (interaction between social groups)	Cognitive Dissonance (cognitive consistency)
Attribution Theory (explaining others' behavior)	Classical/Scientific/Bureaucratic/Human Resources Management (approaches to management and org structure)	Cultivation (TV effects)	Communication Accommodation (whether and how we adapt in interactions)	Compliance Gaining (specific strategies for influencing others)
Communication Privacy Management (how we manage private and public information)	Interaction Process Analysis (contributions of group members)	Cultural Studies (media effects on society; pop culture)	Face Negotiation Theory (management of self esteem needs)	Dramatism (rhetorical tactics like identification and guilt)
Constructivism (cognitive complexity and person-centered messages)	Cultural Theory (how organizations develop and maintain a unique culture)	Media Ecology (the impact of media channels on individuals and society)	Genderlect Styles (how and why men and women communicate differently)	Elaboration Likelihood Model (how people think about messages and the resulting attitude change)
Coordinated Management of Meaning (how we co-construct meaning in interactions)	Functional Theory (functions groups need to fulfill)	Semiotics (the study of the use of signs and symbols)	Muted Group Theory (how people, like women, are silenced)	The Narrative Paradigm (how and why people learn, construct, and judge stories to make decisions)
Dialogic Theory (communicating inclusively)	Groupthink (group cohesion and bad decision making)	Social Cognitive Theory (learning behaviors from media characters)	Speech Codes Theory (how and why different social/cultural groups develop ways of communicating)	The Rhetoric (Aristotle) (different types of persuasive proof, types of speeches, and methods of speech building)

Interpersonal	Group/Organizational	Mass/New Media	Intercultural/Gender	Persuasion/Rhetoric/PR
Expectancy Violations Theory (what happens when our expectations are violated)	Information Systems Theory (how organizations develop rules for handling uncertainty)	Social Information Processing (relationship development online)	Social Identity Theory (differences in group status and behaviors toward outgroups)	Social Judgment Theory (how people respond to persuasive attempts)
Goals-Plans-Actions (how people formulate messages based on goals and scripts)	Input-Process-Output Theory (looks at the conditions, processes, and outcomes of group processes)	Spiral of Silence (explains why and when people are likely to express and withhold their opinions)	Standpoint Theory (explains how we are socialized into ways of knowing based on gender)	Sleeper Effects (explains the implications for "forgetting" information and being persuaded after a time lapse)
Interpersonal Deception Theory (indicators of lying and deception)	Symbolic Convergence Theory (development of code words and shared meanings)	Diffusion of Innovations (the process of learning about and adopting new technology)	Feminist Studies (explores gender depictions, gender roles, and women's issues, etc.)	Theory of Planned Behavior (explains how attitudes, norms, and self efficacy determine behavior)
Relational Dialectics (describes ongoing tensions present in relationships)	X, Y Theory of Management (perceptions of worker motivation and resulting managerial strategies)	Uses & Gratifications (motives for and uses of different media)	Marxist Theory (focus on class and social structure)	Stages of Change (audience-centered look at where people are in the process of persuasion)
Social Exchange Theory (looks at the rewards and costs in relationships)	Theory Z of Management (a humanistic approach to management that slowly develops employees over the long-term)	Framing (how news media presents issues and affects how people interpret those issues)	Meaning of Meaning (describes how meaning is often lost in interactions due to different interpretations)	Attitude Functions (the view that attitudes serve different functions, or uses, for different people)
Social Penetration Theory (looks at self-disclosure at different stages of relationship development)	Network Theory (organizations as complex, multi-level systems)	Media Dependency (how situations and events make people dependent on the media)	Cross Cultural Adaptation Theory (how people adjust when in a new culture)	Image Repair Theory (PR strategies used when there is a crisis or wrongdoing)

(Continued)

Table 1.3 (Continued)

Interpersonal	Group/Organizational	Mass/New Media	Intercultural/Gender	Persuasion/Rhetoric/PR
Symbolic Interactionism (how meaning about the self and others develops through interaction)	Symbolic Convergence Theory (when groups create collective fantasies to build cohesion)	Medium Theory (the effects of channel on reception)	Identity Management Theory (our cultural and relational identities and how to manage them when interacting with others)	Extended Parallel Process Model (how people respond to fear appeals and what fear appeals should include)
Two-Step Flow (the role of interpersonal communication in voting decisions)				
Uncertainty Reduction Theory (strategies to reduce and implications of feeling uncertain in relationships)				
Cognitive Valence Theory (explains the role of intimacy in relationships)				
Politeness Theory (strategies for preserving our own or others' self-esteem in interactions)				

So, looking at these theories and thinking again about our desire to figure out how to get our students involved in politics, a couple of theories could be useful. Specifically, Uses and Gratifications Theory could explain the lack of motivation that leads to reduced involvement in political information. Also, the Theory of Planned Behavior could explain why our students may not be interested in participating in politics. So, we could look at the research on both of these theories for information and insight.

Resources to Consult for Overviews of Communication Theories

- Griffin, E. (2012). *A first look at communication theory* (8th Ed.). New York: McGraw Hill. http://www.afirstlook.com/book

- Infante, D., Rancer, A., & Avtgis, T. (2010). *Contemporary communication theory*. Dubuque, IA: Kendall Hunt. http://www.kendallhunt.com/infante/

- Littlejohn, S. W., & Foss, S. J. (2011). *Theories of human communication* (10th Ed.). Long Grove, IL: Waveland. http://books.google.com/books/about/Theories_of_Human_Communication.html?id=r3Fk0aRpJM4C

- West, R., & Turner, L. H. (2010). *Introducing communication theory: Analysis and application* (4th Ed.). New York: McGraw Hill. http://highered.mcgraw-hill.com/sites/0767430344/information_center_view0/

- Littlejohn, S. W., & Foss, K. A. (2009). *Encyclopedia of communication theory*. Thousand Oaks, CA: Sage. http://knowledge.sagepub.com/view/communicationtheory/SAGE.xml

Resources for communication theory overviews

In sum, to explore our topic we do the following:

1. Start the project by considering what communication context we want to research.
2. Narrow that context to a specific area of study.
3. Find specific concepts we are most interested in by brainstorming and mapping our interests.
4. Conduct cursory searches of the literature to find variable names.
5. Determine if there is a theory that may help us explore our topic.

C. Pose an Interesting, Important Question

We refer to research as "inquiry" because it should be guided by carefully reasoned, interesting questions. Babbie (2004) warned that there are errors in the beginning stages of inquiry that can undermine research projects: inaccurate observations, overgeneralization, selective observation, and illogical reasoning. We will look at each of these in turn to explain why we begin our research projects with a question and an open mind:

- **Inaccurate observations**: We often misremember things or fail to recall things fully, and so our individual observations of human behavior are incomplete. In social science and humanities fields, like communication, we have to make careful, planned observations. So, what we *believe* to be true about human communication may prove to be *untrue*.
- **Overgeneralization**: When we do observe something a couple of times, we tend to infer a pattern. So, we tend to reach conclusions about things based on relatively little information. In social science, we only make generalizations about things once they have been carefully and broadly observed.
- **Selective observations**: Once we have made up our minds about how things are, we tend to look for information that confirms our hunch. In research, on the other hand, we need to look at both confirming and disconfirming information.
- **Illogical reasoning**: Many of our behaviors and beliefs are illogical, but we manage to explain them away, even when faced with contradictory or competing evidence. Once we've made up our minds about how things are, we will use illogical reasoning, such as "the exception proves the rule," to reason away disconfirming information (p. 9).

Clearly, our expectations and beliefs are not a reliable basis for reaching conclusions. For example, we may *expect* that political activities are increasingly done via computer-mediated communication. We may feel very justified for expecting this: We ourselves and all of our friends may use CMC to follow politics (which may be an inaccurate observation), and so we assume everyone does the same (overgeneralization). Therefore, we would look for research that confirms our hunch (selective observation) and discount research that doesn't confirm our belief as methodologically faulty because it doesn't fit our experiences (illogical reasoning). Therefore, to avoid these pitfalls, we *pose a question* rather than seek to confirm a hunch.

We have to be open to the possibility that there is no evidence to support our hunch that students aren't interested in politics or that new media may be a good way to get them involved. It is only after reading, synthesizing, and critiquing the research that exists on a topic—all of which we cover in this book—that we can develop conclusions about our topic. Even then, our conclusions are tentative.

The question you pose at the outset of the project sets up how you will approach the rest of your project. It will decide what you look for in the literature, what you take notes on, how you organize your paper, and the conclusions you reach. We consider the types of questions one might ask in the next section.

1. Types of Questions: Fact, Value, and Policy

Generally, we ask three types of questions in communication research: questions of fact (what is), value (what should be), and policy (what we should do) (Hocking, Stacks, & McDermott, 2003). We also ask questions of definition when we explain the variables in our research, which is addressed in the next section.

Table 1.4   Three Types of Communication Research Questions

	Questions of Fact	Questions of Value	Questions of Policy
Definition	*Questions about objective reality*	*Questions about what is or is not good, moral, right, just, and valuable*	*Questions about what should or should not be done*
Method	These are typically empirical questions that can be answered using objective observation.	These are humanistic questions that are answered using rhetorical, critical, qualitative, or historical methods.	These questions are both empirical and humanistic, as they require us to consider both facts and values.
Example	Are younger people less politically involved?	What types of political content are most involving?	What can we do to get more people interested in politics?

It's helpful when considering how you are going to approach your topic to consider what type of question is going to be most interesting to you personally and most relevant to modern society. Consider the many different types of questions you can ask about facts, values, and policies when you're thinking about how you want to approach your topic. Do you want to describe the current state of knowledge? Then that is likely a question of fact. Do you want to evaluate or critique communication? That is likely going to come from a question of value. Do you want to recommend particular behaviors, or discourage other behaviors? Those are questions of policy. Almost any topic can be looked at from any one of these angles. In the next section, we consider how to choose the question that will contribute the most to our understanding of communication processes.

Common Mistake

Avoid asking loaded questions that assume what you will find. This opens us up to problems with confirmation bias. For example, asking, "Why is political news so biased?" is a loaded question because it assumes that news © Robert Jakatics, 2014. Shutterstock, Inc. is biased. Instead, we would ask, "Is there evidence of bias in political news?"

Choose an Important Question

Research is only useful if it answers a question that is important to ourselves and other people. Think about the classes you've taken in college—the ones that were the best were likely the ones that were most practical and relevant to your goals and interests. The classes you liked the least were probably the ones that did not seem relevant. Choose a question that is important to you personally, and to the health, well-being, and lives of other people. Choosing something important will keep your interest in the topic sparked throughout the process of reading and writing, and it will also make your paper more interesting to read.

D. Define Target Variables

1. Independent and Dependent Variables

Once we know what has been studied and what we are interested in within a given context, we can start to think about the specifics of what we want to study by deciding on a couple of specific variables. Variables are either independent or dependent. **Independent variables affect other variables**. Gender is an independent variable because it affects communication. It has been found to influence nonverbal decoding, use of nonverbal and verbal communication, and communication tactics. Similarly, age, traits, personality types, relationship types, etc., are typically independent variables as they are something that cannot be manipulated or changed by the researcher.

Dependent variables, on the other hand, are the variables that are changed, predicted, or affected by independent variables. Put another way, dependent variables *depend on* independent variables. The communication tactics a person uses in a conversation, for example, *depend on* their personality and gender. Similarly, the maintenance behaviors we use in a relationship *depend on* gender, personality, and how we feel about the relationship. As another example, the media we use depends on our personality and communication needs.

So, using age as an example, that is an independent variable because it cannot be changed, but it affects other variables. Political involvement, on the other hand, is an outcome variable in this scenario because it may *depend on* age.

2. Reportative, Stipulative, and Operational Definitions

In addition to understanding the types of variables we are looking at, we also have to consider carefully how we define and use variable names. As mentioned in the previous section, we often name concepts and variables in particular ways in communication. We also define them and measure them in ways that are in keeping with those academic definitions.

Hocking et al. (2002) distinguish between reportive definitions and stipulative definitions. **Reportive definitions** are the customary, or common, definition of a term that we would find in a dictionary. **Stipulative definitions**, on the other hand, are the definitions we offer for variables in academic research. Authors will often offer a stipulative definition in the literature review of their paper to explain how they intend to use a term throughout their paper.

In the method section, authors will often explain how they measured a variable on a scale, how they manipulated a variable in an experiment, or what they looked for in the content they analyzed: this is the **operational definition**. Ideally, stipulative and operational definitions are closely related.

Common Mistake

Many times, students will use a dictionary or dictionary websites when defining variables for their papers. But the dictionary definition and the definition used in research can be very different. When writing an *academic* paper, use the *academic* definition. You can often find the academic definition in textbooks and research articles.

© Robert Jakatics, 2014. Shutterstock, Inc.

We have to look closely at the definitions of our concepts and variables when we are in the early stages of focusing our topic: Are these common variables in research? Are these the variables we intend to study? What type of variable is this? How might my variables and concepts fit together?

In summary, to formulate our problem question, we:

1. Consider whether we are interested in questions of fact, value, or policy.
2. Use our concepts and variables to formulate a question.
3. Check definitions of concepts and variables to consider how they may be related to each other.

REFERENCES

Babbie, E. R. (2010). *The practice of social research* (12th ed). Belmont, CA: Cengage.

Hendrick, C., Hendrick, S., & Dicke, A. (1998). The love attitudes scale: Short form. *Journal of Personal and Social Relationships, 15*, 147–159.

Hocking, J. E., Stacks, D. W., & McDermott, S. T. (2002). *Communication research* (3rd ed). Boston: Pearson.

Kerlinger, F. N., & Lee, H. B. (2000). *Foundations of behavioral research* (4th ed.). New York: Harcourt.

Lee, J. A. (1973). *Colours of love: An exploration of the ways of loving.* Toronto: New Press.

ACTIVITIES

1. Brainstorming Exercise

1. Choose one context of study in communication.
2. Brainstorm concepts that are of interest to you in that context.
3. Organize concepts into these categories:
   a. Source
   b. Message
   c. Channel
   d. Receiver
   e. Outcomes
4. Choose concepts from two or more of these categories that you think are a) interesting, b) related to each other, and c) would be practical to study.

2. Mapping to Explore Your Topic

If you are struggling to find a direction, sometimes brainstorming and mind-mapping can help you discover focused areas of research to explore.

1. Choose a communication context.
2. Brainstorm all of the concepts you would be interested in studying within that context.

3. Organize concepts into categories that fit together.
4. Choose the category of concepts that is most interesting to you.

3. Try Out Different Questions

Use the concepts you chose in Activity 2 to formulate a series of questions. Phrase your topic as a question of fact, then a question of value, then a question of policy. From the questions you developed, which sounds most important to you personally? To society? To academic researchers?

For example, for a paper on cultivation of inaccurate perceptions that people learn from TV, we might ask:

- Are there cultivation effects of viewing reality TV? (fact)
- Are the lessons taught in reality TV immoral? (value)
- How might we use reality TV programming to promote public health or other prosocial behaviors? (policy)

4. Reportative, Stipulative, and Operational Definitions

Compare the www.dictionary.com definition of your concepts versus the concept definitions found in communication textbooks. Find a measure of that concept in communication research. How are these definitions similar and different? Are you sure, based on the stipulative and operational definitions, that this is the concept you are interested in studying?

Dictionary.com site

5. Recommended Assignment

Formulate one research question to guide your paper. Explain whether it is a question of fact, value, or policy and justify your decision to ask this type of question. List 2 to 3 communication concepts, or specific variables, related to your question and give the stipulative definition of each concept and variable from either a textbook or other academic source.

EXAMPLE COMPLETED STEP 1

1. General Context: Political Communication

2. Mind Map to Consider Concepts:

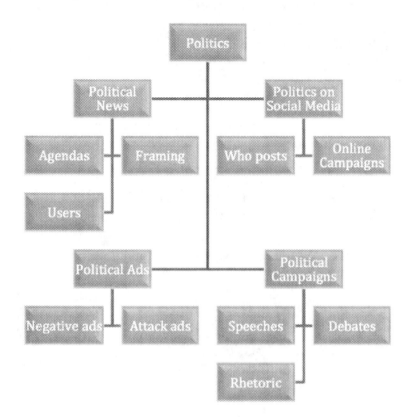

3. Questions I Could Ask:

- How does the news cover politics? (fact)
- What strategies should be used to reach potential voters? (policy)
- What individual characteristics are related to political involvement? (fact)
- Why do people vote? (fact)
- Are certain political ads unethical? (value)

My Problem Question:

How can we get more people involved in politics? (policy)

4. Concepts Related to My Problem Question:

For example, for "involvement," dictionary.com gives this definition:

in·volve

1. to include as a necessary circumstance, condition, or consequence; imply; entail: This job involves long hours and hard work.
2. to engage or employ.
3. to affect, as something within the scope of operation.
4. to include, contain, or comprehend within itself or its scope.
5. to bring into an intricate or complicated form or condition.
6. to bring into difficulties (usually followed by with): a plot to involve one nation in a war with another.
7. to cause to be troublesomely associated or concerned, as in something embarrassing or unfavorable: Don't involve me in your quarrel!
8. to combine inextricably (usually followed by with).
9. to implicate, as in guilt or crime, or in any matter or affair.
10. to engage the interests or emotions or commitment of: to become involved in the disarmament movement; to become involved with another woman.
11. to preoccupy or absorb fully (usually used passively or reflexively): You are much too involved with the problem to see it clearly.
12. to envelop or enfold, as if with a wrapping.
13. to swallow up, engulf, or overwhelm.
14. a. Archaic. to roll, surround, or shroud, as in a wrapping. b. to roll up on itself; wind spirally; coil; wreathe.
    http://dictionary.reference.com/browse/involvement?s=t

Definition of involve

Perse defined involvement as mental involvement, or mentally engaging and thinking about the media content we consume. Perse (1990) developed an involvement scale that focused on cognitive elaboration, or how much people pay attention to and think about media content. It includes:

- Thinking about what content means to me
- Thinking about how content relates to what I know
- Thinking about what the content means to others
- Thinking about the content over and over again
- Thinking about what should be done

The reportative definition and stipulative definition are subtly different. The dictionary.com definition focuses on general engagement, emotional engagement and interest, and preoccupation. Some elements of this definition are in Perse's operationalization of involvement, which focuses on people's thoughts about personal relevance, personal knowledge, meaning to self and others, and preoccupation.

Perse, E. M. (1990). Involvement with local television news: Cognitive and emotional dimensions. *Human Communication Research, 16,* 556–581.

STEP 2

The Second Step in Your Investigation:
Look for Clues in the Academic Literature

As your investigation begins, it is important to consider all of the places you can look for clues, to consider the types of clues you need to solve the puzzle, and to be able to evaluate the quality of the evidence you find. This chapter discusses numerous strategies for finding evidence for your investigation via both academic and nonacademic resources.

THIS CHAPTER COVERS:

A. Understand the Quality and Types of Sources Available
    1. Evaluating Sources
    2. Types of Sources
B. Search for Sources
    1. Finding Academic Research
    2. Use Your Library to Find Print Sources
    3. Search the Internet

Finding academic sources can be a challenging experience for students who typically rely on Google, Yahoo!, or Bing to find information. Think of searching for sources like conducting an investigation. You will have to try numerous strategies, look in different places, and follow different leads to ultimately find the best sources for your project. You have to consider the evidence you find in light of the source: Can you rely on it? Is it relevant to your investigation? Does it fit with other evidence you've seen? This section overviews some strategies for collecting the best available evidence.

A. Understand the Quality and Types of Sources Available

1. Evaluating Sources

When citing information, your credibility as a writer is dependent upon the credibility of your sources. If you cite incorrect, old, or biased information in your literature review, the reader of that work will assume that you did not evaluate the sources properly. When it comes to credibility, not all sources are created equal. Using the **TRAACC method** to track down the best sources will help build a strong argument within your paper. Regardless of the type of source you choose, there are a few key considerations you should keep in mind:

T: The **type** of source
R: The **relevance** of the source
A: The **author**
A: The **aim** of the source
C: The nature of the **content**
C: The **currency**

In addition to these considerations, this section will outline the various types of support you might consult to gain information. These include books, academic journals, popular press, and websites. We will review the advantages and disadvantages of each medium as well.

The Type of source. One of the first considerations you should make regarding a potential source of information is what kind of source you are reading. There are two basic types: primary and secondary. A **primary source** is the original source of information. Think of this as an "eye witness account." This means that the author of the material you are reading directly observed the information they are reporting. One example of a primary source is an empirical journal article. Empirical journal articles are ones where a researcher or researchers conducted a study and reported their direct observations. Another example of a primary source would be an eyewitness to an event telling their story to a reporter. The eyewitness is a primary source—they directly observed the event and are therefore credible to speak about it.

Overall, primary sources report new ideas or discoveries. There is little to no outside interpretation present in primary sources. Because of this fact, primary sources are more desired when citing information. You as the writer can clearly comprehend what the original author was reporting and use that information to support the claims you wish to make in your literature review.

Secondary sources are sources that compile or interpret primary sources. Secondary sources do not provide new information themselves. This does not mean that secondary sources are not credible; however, more careful scrutiny of secondary sources is typically needed in order to deem them as credible. Textbooks are typically secondary sources, because they compile information from primary sources. Textbooks are often considered credible sources; the information found there is not wrong, per se. However, there is still interpretation that is involved in consolidating information into a textbook chapter. What is included, emphasized, and omitted is up to the authors and publishers of the text.

Encyclopedias are another type of secondary source. One encyclopedia that is often used is Wikipedia. Wikipedia is an online, open source database of knowledge. Anyone can create, edit, or delete information on Wikipedia. This brings the credibility of Wikipedia into question. The information you find on this site is typically correct, but you never want to cite it in academic or professional settings. Falsehoods can be deliberately created and information may not be complete.

Overall, secondary sources should be avoided when citing in your literature review. Essentially, you are relying on someone else's interpretation when reading secondary sources. So why should you ever consult a secondary source? Secondary sources are invaluable to getting a sense for your topic or for finding primary sources. Consider Wikipedia. A good Wikipedia site will give you an overview of a topic and should include links to original sources. The same is true for a textbook. Reading a textbook will give you a good grasp of the types of search terms, concepts, and in some cases, a bibliography of primary sources for you to consult. Whenever possible, seek out the original primary source for your own paper.

Helpful Tip

Use secondary sources in the beginning of your search to gain general knowledge of your topic and to help find primary sources.

Always cite primary sources when available to enhance your credibility as a writer.

© iQoncept, 2014. Shutterstock, Inc.

Table 2.1 Examples of Sources

Primary Sources	Secondary Sources
Empirical Research	Criticisms
Speeches	Commentaries
Diaries	Textbooks
Official Records (court documents, etc.)	Encyclopedias
Interviews	Bibliographies
Works of Art	Biographies

The Relevance of the source. When searching for sources, you will most likely come across several types of information that you might use. You want to be sure you choose the best, most relevant information to support your points. When you are conducting your search, you can begin assessing the relevance of a source by looking at the summary or abstract that is given. Summaries included in search engine results or in academic databases can help you make a quick assessment of how useful this piece of information might be to your project. Summaries and abstracts often include the method of inquiry (what type of methodology was used), the theory or approach that was used in the study, and any main concepts or variables that were examined.

However, don't stop at the abstract or summary. Abstracts are written by authors to summarize major findings and to enhance interest in the paper. They are typically about 250 words. Given the length of a journal article (up to 25 or 30 pages), you can imagine that not everything the article accomplishes is evident in the abstract. Reading the actual content is going to be the best way to assess whether an article does actually support your position. But a quick review of the abstract is a good starting point to determine the relevance of a source before investing time and effort in reading the full report.

Another consideration when deciding relevance is the intended audience of the source. Sources like newspapers and some websites are tailored for a mass, general audience. The language used and the type of information included in these sources is written at about a high-school level and tends to be more general in scope. Other sources like academic articles are intended for a more highly educated audience. Some professors might require you to use only academic sources like books and journal articles because they tend to be more specific in scope.

Another way to be sure you are including relevant material is to be sure to complete a thorough search. If you use Google Scholar and type in the keywords "uncertainty reduction theory," you will get thousands of entries. Don't just choose the first five articles that you see; be diligent. Use multiple databases, search terms, and sources to find the best information. Internet search engines are the fastest way to find information, but they do not always turn up the most relevant sources. Spending more time on your search will help you in the long run, because you will have better quality sources and you are less likely to have to go back and search again if the information you turn up is not good.

Helpful Tip

Always look at your research questions or hypotheses when deciding if a source is relevant. In the first step, you specified concepts, variables, and theories that were relevant to your problem question. You want to make sure that all of your sources can help you answer your problem question by focusing on sources that address the specific variables, concepts, and / or theory that interests you.

© doomu, 2014. Shutterstock, Inc.

The Author. When choosing sources, another factor that you should consider is the author of the material you are reading. All credible sources of information should provide author credentials that can clue you in to how credible that source might be. For example, authors will often tell you if they have particular expertise to enhance their credibility. They might list degrees earned or experience that might make them particularly knowledgeable about a topic. For example, a cancer survivor who writes a book about his or her experiences has credibility to speak on that topic.

When seeking sources for literature reviews, you will be primarily searching academic sources. Experts in communication often possess a master's or doctorate degree. They might work in higher education, government agencies, or private companies. You can find research that is published in books, journal articles, and in some cases, on websites. If you cannot identify the author of a study that you are reading, it is probably not a good idea to cite that information.

Some groups like the Pew Research Center employ several experts to research various topics. They report their findings on their website, but some of their articles do not have an author. Does that mean that you shouldn't believe what they report? Not entirely. Organizations like Pew typically have an "about us" page that you can click on that shows who is responsible for the content on the page. As with print sources, websites should clearly detail who is creating or posting content and what their credentials are for doing so.

The Aim of the source. The **aim**, or purpose, of the source tells you their reason for putting information out to the public. When determining the aim of a source, consider factors such as a mission statement, the intended audience, and any sponsorships or advertisements present. If you are reading research on a website sponsored by the tobacco industry about the ineffectiveness of PSAs about smoking, you should carefully consider that information. Sponsorships and advertisers may sway publishers of content to make the sponsor look good. This might not always be the case, but it is a fact that should be taken into consideration when citing information from sources that may be profit driven.

This is one reason why you can generally trust academic journal articles. The purpose of an academic journal article is to disseminate ideas and research to other interested parties. People who write academic journal articles often do so without any monetary gain. Some authors may receive grant funding to complete research studies, but that should be disclosed in the article so that you can take that information into consideration when judging the credibility of the research.

The nature of the Content. In addition to the aim of the source, you want to consider the accuracy and bias within the content. There are many ways to assess both accuracy and bias. With regards to accuracy, one of the best ways to tell if information is accurate is to compare it to other known sources. Does the information stated in this source seem similar to what you've already found? If so, then it may be accurate. If not, you may have to dig a bit further to determine accuracy.

One of the best ways to determine accuracy is to verify the information by checking out cited sources. When an author provides you with citations, they are acknowledging where they got their information and offering a chance for you as the reader to find that information as well. You can assess the credibility of the sources as well; if an author uses credible sources to support their claims, you can probably trust the accuracy of their work.

Another content issue that you should observe is whether the information presented seems biased. Bias can be observed by considering whether the information is subjective or objective. **Objective writing** is free of opinion. Empirical research studies are considered objective; the author is making an observation based on research that was conducted. **Subjective writing** contains author opinions or perspectives. Subjective writing may not be biased; authors might present both sides of an issue in a fair manner. However, if an article appears to cover only one perspective, care should be taken when citing this information.

The Currency of the source. The last consideration you should make when choosing a good source is the currency of the material, or when it was published. Typically, the most recent material is the most desirable. However, this is not always the case. For example, if you were writing a paper on a theory, you might want to include the seminal piece, or the first article or book written on a topic. In some cases, the seminal work might still be relevant today, even if it was written thirty years ago.

The time frame in terms of the exact date of a source is sometimes less important than shifts in thinking. Academic sources may still be relevant, even if they are ten years old. Theories tend not to shift very often; you want to be sure you are using information that supports the current way of thinking. You can determine this by completing a thorough literature search. Read carefully through the literature review section. The author(s) should clearly detail how they are using any theoretical perspectives or variables of interest.

This is not to say that the publication date of information is not important. On the contrary, some types of information are highly time-sensitive. Local and international news, health information, technology advancements, and even political issues can change within a very small time frame. What might have been legal one day can be illegal the next, and vice versa. Again, completing a thorough search of information will help you stay current and avoid misinformation in your argument.

When citing information, you want to be sure to look for the publication date. Books, journal articles, newspapers, and magazines will almost always include a publication date either before an article or in the front matter (table of contents, preface, etc.). Websites should have a "last-updated" date on the page (usually at the bottom) or a copyright date. Or, you can tell if a website is regularly maintained if the information presented is current (posted newsletters, blog posts, recent news articles, etc.).

STEP 2

Caution

If you cannot find any publication date (or evidence of recent activity on a website), you may not want to use that source. Carefully consider the other criteria discussed to make an educated decision regarding the quality of the information.

© Thomas Pajot, 2014. Shutterstock, Inc.

2. Types of Sources

When searching for sources, you always want to consult your instructor. She or he may have specific guidelines that may limit the types of sources you may use (i.e., no websites, academic journals only, etc.). Below is a list of the types of sources you might use to construct your literature review.

Academic journals. When constructing a literature review, most likely you will cite academic journal articles. Journal articles are often held in higher regard within the social sciences than other sources due to the **peer review process**. The process of peer review is complex and sometimes very difficult. During this process, an editor and two or more "blind" reviewers read, evaluate, and make recommendations for accepting, revising, or rejecting an article. The reviewers are experts in the area of study, and can therefore judge the quality of the research presented for review. An academic journal article typically goes through this process at least twice before it is published. Therefore, the content is expected to be very high quality compared to content that is openly reviewed by only one or two book editors or book reviewers. That is why peer reviewed publications are held in such high esteem: they are rigorously evaluated and difficult to achieve.

That being said, not all academic journals are equally credible. There are increasing numbers of for-profit corporations that own and/or distribute journals, vanity publications (where you can independently publish your work without peer review), and pay-for-publication outlets that may not have such strict guidelines for publication. How do you know if the journal is rigorous? Here are a few tips: First, look at the acceptance rates. Extremely high acceptance rates mean that the journal may not get enough submissions to be picky. Many, but not all, journals also have an "Impact Factor" rating, which can tell you how influential publications from a particular journal are. We can also look at who publishes the journal. Communication organizations throughout the United States have their own journals. Here are the current journals published by the international, national, and regional Communication Associations:

Major Publications from Communication Associations:

- National Communication Association Journals:
  www.natcom.org/journals.aspx

  - *Communication and Critical / Cultural Studies*
  - *Communication Education*
  - *Communication Monographs*
  - *Communication Teacher*
  - *Critical Studies in Media Communication*
  - *Journal of International and Intercultural Communication*
  - *Journal of Applied Communication Research*
  - *Quarterly Journal of Speech*
  - *Review of Communication*
  - *Text and Performance Quarterly*

- Association for Education in Journalism and Mass
  Communication: http://www.aejmc.org/home/publications/

  - *Journal of Advertising Education*
  - *Communication Methods and Measures*
  - *Journal of Communication Inquiry*
  - *Electronic News*
  - *International Communication Research Journal*
  - *Communication Law and Policy*
  - *Journal of magazine and New Media Research*
  - *Mass Communication and Society*
  - *Journal of Mass Media Ethics*
  - *Newspaper Research Journal*
  - *Journal of Public Relations Research*
  - *Visual Communication Quarterly*
  - *Journal of Media and Religion*

- Broadcast Education Association:
  http://beaweb.org/publications.htm

  - *Journal of Broadcasting & Electronic Media*
  - *Journal of Radio & Audio Media*
  - *Journal of Media Education*

- International Communication Association Journals:
  http://www.icahdq.org/pubs/journals.asp

  - *Journal of Communication*
  - *Human Communication Research*
  - *Communication Theory*
  - *Journal of Computer-Mediated Communication*
  - *Communication, Culture, & Critique*

- Eastern Communication Association Journals:
  http://ecasite.org/aws/ECA/pt/sp/p_pubs_main
  - *Communication Quarterly*
  - *Communication Research Reports*
  - *Qualitative Research Reports in Communication*

- Western Communication Association Journals:
  http://www.westcomm.org
  - *Western Journal of Communication*
  - *Communication Reports*

- Southern States Communication Association Journal:
  http://www.ssca.net/publications
  - *Southern Communication Journal*

- Central States Communication Association Journal:
  http://www.csca-net.org/aws/CSCA/pt/sp/journal
  - *Communication Studies*

- Northwest Communication Association:
  http://www.northwestcomm.org/?page_id=14
  - *The Northwest Journal of Communication*

It should be pointed out that there are many rigorous, high-impact journals that are not published by communication associations. The National Communication Association maintains a list of 105 journals with their associated impact ratings: http://www.natcom.org/Secondary.aspx?id=122&terms=105%20Communication%20Journals

NCA's Research and
Publishing Resource Center

Books. If your professor allows you to use books in your paper, there are numerous types of books that can be useful to you for different reasons throughout your project: textbooks, handbooks, academic studies, and academic reference books. Most books written for student and academic audiences are reviewed by editors and experts in the field, so these types of books tend to be more rigorously fact-checked compared to popular press books.

Textbooks are a place to turn when you need help with definitions of concepts or explanations of theories. **Textbooks** are secondary sources that are written to introduce students to an area of study or specific skill set, so the authors often summarize the research available on relevant communication concepts or theories. That being said, textbooks can be a great resource to find a) clear, succinct explanations of concepts and theories related to your topic; b) information about the prominent researchers and theorists who are conducting studies related to your topic; and c) an overview of how the concepts and theories have developed and changed over time. Therefore, textbooks can be a great starting point for helping you find direction when writing your paper.

Handbooks, on the other hand, tend to have more detailed information on a more narrow topic of interest. There are handbooks available in communication studies on each of the primary contexts of study. Though, like a textbook, handbooks are secondary sources, each chapter is typically written by an expert who conducts research in a narrow area of study. Therefore, you may find it helpful to read a chapter in a handbook that is related to your topic. Handbook chapters often provide valuable information about a) the history of theories and concepts; b) the most recent research conducted on a theory or concept; and c) critiques, evaluations, and directions for future research. This, too, may help you find articles for your own paper and offer you some context, or background knowledge, that will be helpful as you read the literature and write your paper.

A handbook is typically an edited book, but there are other types of very topic-specific edited books available through the library. **Edited books** are when a collection of topically related essays or studies, written by researchers and theorists in the field, are in one book edited by one or more subject experts. Chapters in edited books may be a primary source if they are reporting the results of a study, or they may be secondary sources if they are providing a critique or review of existing research. The type of information you may glean from an edited book depends on the type of content covered in the chapters.

Other academic books are similarly diverse: some books report on a study or series of studies, some are reviews, critiques, or syntheses of existing research. Many of the most prominent researchers for our popular theories have books and / or book chapters that they have written to justify, explain, or contextualize their theorizing. These types of books can be very helpful to you as you write your paper, as they often offer the most in-depth discussion of theories, concepts, and research methods.

Popular press. The popular press includes sources such as magazines and news outlets. Popular press sources can be very helpful to get recent information on a topic, because they are published much more frequently than academic articles. The worthiness of these types of sources often varies, due to the fact that not all authors who write articles are subject area experts. Popular press sources are often for-profit, which means they exist to make money. Because of this fact, they often have less stature and credibility than academic journal articles. However, they can be very useful to demonstrate the importance or prevalence of a particular issue you might be researching.

National newspapers and news outlets like the *New York Times, USA Today, CNN,* and *Fox News* tend to have a more credible reputation due to their high reporting standards and quality of reporters. However, some types of news tend to be more credible than others. For example, there are two types of news stories: hard news and soft news. **Hard news** covers events and stories that are happening at the moment. These stories often have important political or social value, and reporters tend to focus on the factual nature of the event. **Soft news** is not time-centered, in that these stories could be placed or aired in the news at any time. Soft news often focuses on human-interest stories like celebrity gossip, advice columns, and opinion pieces. The goal of this type of story is to entertain. As you can imagine, hard news stories are often given more importance than soft news. This doesn't mean that information presented in soft news is less credible; it just means a more critical eye should be used when citing that information.

Magazines might also be important sources for information on a current issue. Popular magazines like *Time* and *Newsweek* can cover stories in a more lengthy manner than news outlets like *USA Today.* As with news sources, the author of a magazine article might not be a subject expert. Some magazines cover both hard and soft news; other magazines (like *People*) focus primarily on soft news. **Trade magazines** are designed to give information tailored to a particular profession. These publications have a specific audience in mind, and tend to publish articles that only pertain to that audience. *Advertising Age,* for example, publishes stories related to those who are in the advertising business. Trade publications often include specific information that might be helpful when discussing any technological or practical issues related to a topic.

Table 2.2 Frequently Used Popular Press Sources

Broadcast News	Newspapers	Popular & Trade Magazines
CBS News www.cbsnews.com	*Los Angeles Times* www.latimes.com	*Advertising Age* www.adage.com
CNN www.cnn.com	*New York Times* www.nytimes.com	*Broadcasting & Cable* www.broadcastingcable.com/
Fox News www.foxnews.com	*USA Today* www.usatoday.com	*Newsweek* www.newsweek.com
NBC News www.nbcnews.com	*Wall Street Journal* www.wsj.com	*Time* www.time.com
ABC News www.abc.go.com	*Washington Post* www.washingtonpost.com	*US News and World Report* www.usnews.com

Websites. Obviously, there is a lot of information (and misinformation) available online. The criteria for evaluating sources can be particularly helpful when considering whether a website is a useful, quality source of information. Remembering the TRAACC method for evaluating sources is particularly helpful when using websites in your literature review. There are also details specific to websites that you can scrutinize to consider the type and quality of the information (Online Library Learning Center, n.d.):

1. Check the Universal Resource Link (URL), or website address. Determine if the root address (the homepage for the website) is a good source or not. For example, the website http://drcurnalia.wordpress.com/my-forthcoming-book/ has a *root* address of drcurnalia.wordpress.com.

2. Look at the website domain (the suffix at the end of the root address). My personal website, http://drcurnalia. wordpress.com, is a .com domain, which tells you that it is a commercial website. Here is a guide to common U.S. website domains:

Dr. Curnalia's website

- .com: A commercial website
- .edu: A website for a school
- .gov: A government website
- .org: A nonprofit website
- .net: A network website
- .mil: A military website

Generally, .edu and .gov domains are considered the most credible, though there are some nonprofit and commercial websites that we frequently retrieve information from in communication research. As the number and types of domains increase, using domain names as an indicator will get more difficult, and students and professors alike will have to analyze the content of websites closely to consider the quality and reliability of content.

Table 2.3 Frequently Used Web Sources for Communication Scholars

Pew Research Center for People and the Press: http://www.people-press.org/	Pew Internet and American Life Project: http://www.pewinternet.org/

(Continued)

Table 2.3   (Continued)

American National Elections Studies: http://www.electionstudies.org/ 	Gallup: http://www.gallup.com/home.aspx
Searchable Database of Stats Collected by the US Government: http://fedstats.sites.usa.gov 	U.S. Census Bureau: http://www.census.gov/
Centers for Disease Control and Prevention Fast Stats: http://www.cdc.gov/nchs/fastats/Default.htm 	National Center for Health Statistics: http://www.cdc.gov/nchs/
Bureau of Labor Statistics: www.BLS.gov 	Stats for Other Countries: http://www.bls.gov/bls/other.htm

B. Search for Sources

How you go about searching for sources depends on the scope of your literature review. The traditional, **narrative literature review** is most common, and typically summarizes the academic literature relevant to your topic to make critiques and reach conclusions (University of Toledo University Libraries, 2013). These types of literature reviews are typically focused on a narrowly defined subset of articles, but do not necessarily have to be comprehensive. On the other hand, more **systematic literature reviews**, where you are trying to summarize and reach conclusions based on all available research on your topic, and **meta-analysis reviews** where you are using statistics to analyze research results and

Helpful Hints

Check out the University System of Georgia's "Evaluating Internet Information" page for more details about evaluating websites:

http://www.usg.edu/galileo/skills/unit07/internet07_08.phtml

© Odua Images, 2014. Shutterstock, Inc.

reach conclusions, require a comprehensive search of the literature that requires carefully planned searches. The strategies for searching that we cover here will work for any one of these types of literature reviews, though they are most often applied to the narrative literature review.

1. Finding Academic Research

To access academic research, you typically need to use academic research databases, which are often only available through library websites. Databases, unlike search engines, are focused on one type of publication or one discipline. Therefore, you will likely need to use more than one database when searching for literature, as different databases search different collections of books and academic journals.

Table 2.4   Commonly Used Databases in Communication Studies

Database	What It Searches
Academic Search Premier	General publications in numerous disciplines; includes trade publications and popular press
LexisNexis	Newspaper articles from major U.S. newspapers; magazines; broadcast transcripts; State and Federal Court cases
Communication & Mass Media Complete	Academic journals in communication and media studies; some content from psychology
CommAbstracts	Academic journals and books in communication
PsycInfo	Academic journal articles and books in psychology and some in communication
Communication Studies Sage Collection	Full text of Sage's communication journals

Though we access databases differently, databases are similar in their functionality to common search engines: you can use Boolean operators to broaden and narrow your searches, results are listed one page at a time, and you can sort your results by date or relevance. You use the variables you decided to research to begin searching.

In this guide, I will use ERIC as an example. ERIC is a database provided by the U.S. Department of Education, and you may have other options depending on your library's subscriptions.

Here is the search page for ERIC. You have a text box to type your search terms into, including Boolean operators. You also have various other limiters you can set, including limiting results to only peer reviewed articles, or searching for articles available as full text.

ERIC Database

Generally, the first search you use should be simple. You use your chosen variables to create a search phrase, or a phrase that you use to look for relevant articles in the databases. The search phrase should include simple terms, avoid complicated phrases, eliminate unnecessary words, remove unnecessary prefixes and suffixes, and skip unnecessary limiters.

Example of a BAD search phrase:
political engagement among young people

Example of a GOOD search phrase:
political engagement

Why is the second phrase better? Unnecessary words are removed (i.e., "among") and the more common variable name, which we discussed in the last chapter, is used (i.e., "political engagement"). Relatively simple changes like this can vastly improve our search results.

Avoid This Common Mistake

Students often start their projects by entering a long, complicated search phrase into a single search box. Then they get frustrated when they can't find articles. Instead:

© Robert Jakatics, 2014. Shutterstock, Inc.

- Begin with one or two general communication concepts that you have confirmed by referring to communication textbooks or journal articles.

- Do not include any unnecessary words, like "communication" or any articles (i.e., the, an, a).

- Then get more general or specific depending on what you find.

Having a clear problem question written in advance is essential, as it will be the basis of your search phrase. You should have specific variables relevant to a communication context before you start searching. Also, having gleaned those variables from a quick database search or from communication textbooks, you should be confident that you are using the correct search terms.

So, we will begin with our simple search. This search returned 880 articles.

For each record, you are given the article title, which is a hyperlink to the full record, the source title, the authors' names, and a brief view of the abstract.

Once you have your initial search results, you have a couple of options:

1. *Keep* these results because you have just enough on-topic sources.
2. *Narrow* your search because you found too many articles to go through.
3. *Broaden* your search because you found too few sources.

Narrowing your search after finding too many results. Using this search, we got far too many results to look through. If there are too many results, narrow your search by *adding more terms* linked together with AND. Using "AND" tells the search engine that we want articles that include all of the specific terms in our search phrase. We can also use quotation marks around exact phrases, such as "political engagement," to tell the search engine that we want that exact phrase in the articles.

So, we may narrow the search by adding more specific terms to our search phrase (i.e., "Political engagement" AND youth).

STEP 2

This search took us down to 23 articles related to our research interests, which is a fair number to look through. To further refine our results, we could also use "NOT", which excludes certain terms from our search. So, if we didn't want to look at articles having to do with teaching political engagement in schools, we could search for:

"Political engagement" AND youth NOT classroom

This search took us down to 22 results, which is slowly getting us closer to a reasonable number of articles to look through. Notice too, on the left side of the search screen, that ERIC shows us articles broken down by year of publication, descriptor, and source. Also under the search box, we can limit our results to just peer reviewed articles. Most search engines will provide options such as these so that we can narrow our search results. For example, if we chose to only look at articles since 2005, we would further reduce the number of sources to 17, which is a very manageable number of abstracts to look through. That's a lot better than looking through all 880 original results!

Finding too few results. More commonly, students find that there are too few results with their initial search and, sometimes, they find no sources at all with their first search. There are several possible reasons for this: using the wrong search terms, misspelled terms, having too many search terms, or having too narrow a search phrase. Each of these will be addressed.

Helpful Hints

Before broadening search terms, double-check the following:

- Always *double-check your spelling* before changing your search.
- *Eliminate limiters*. For example, the quotation marks used to phrase-search limit the search to finding that exact phrase, so we can delete those.
- *Eliminate the least important search terms*.
- *Look for synonyms* for your most essential search terms.

© Odua Images, 2014. Shutterstock, Inc.

If we search again and are still finding too few results, we should *eliminate search terms*. Also, eliminate extraneous terms. Often, students will include terms like "communication" in their search phrase. This is not necessary to include, particularly if we're searching in the communication databases, because relatively few articles about communication actually use that term.

If modifications to the original phrase don't work, we may have to modify the words in our search phrase. We can do this first by *truncation*. **Truncation** is removing the suffixes of terms in your search phrase to broaden the search. So, in our search phrase we may have had "political." We can truncate that using an asterisk: politic*. Now, the search engine will look at articles that contain the words politic, politics, political, politicking, etc.

The second change to search terms is to *identify synonyms* for search terms and use "OR". Using OR between similar search terms tells the search engine to return articles that include any of those search terms: age OR youth OR adolescent.

So, our expanded search phrase that includes truncation and "OR" looks like this:

politic* AND (age OR youth OR adolescent)

We put the variations of "youth" in parentheses. When you complete a mathematical equation, you do the math in parentheses first because those numbers belong together. Here, you're telling the computer to look at the terms in parentheses together in much the same way. As expected, this significantly expands our search results: we now have 1,787 results. Using a combination of strategies, we can narrow or expand our results as needed to find articles relevant to our topic.

Table 2.5 Narrowing and Expanding a Search

Search Phrase Operators	Uses
AND	Tells the search engine that you want both of these terms in the article: Ex: television AND news
OR	Tells the search engine that either of the search terms would be acceptable. Used most often for synonyms. Ex: television OR tv
NOT	Tells the search engine you do not want articles with a certain term in them. Ex: television NOT newspaper
Truncation	Tells the search engine to look for variations of a term: Ex: news* tells the search engine to look for news, newspaper, newscast, newscasters, etc.
Phrase-Searching	Tells the search engine that you want articles that contain a specific phrase Ex: "uses and gratifications"
Search Field	Limits the search engine to looking for keywords, phrases, and terms in certain fields or areas of the articles and books.

It is often beneficial to *try another database*. In communication studies, there are several databases available and each searches a specific set of academic journals and books. Each database you use is searching different sources, so your results will change if you move to another database. In ERIC, we are looking at education-related sources. Our results would be different if we were looking in Communication & Mass Media Complete, a commonly used database in the communication discipline. There is a lot of overlap in communication databases, therefore you may consider moving to another discipline's databases, particularly if that discipline studies communication-relevant topics.

Psychology databases can be particularly helpful. I encourage you to search through PsycInfo if you are looking at interpersonal, organizational, persuasion, political, or mass communication, as a lot of communication theories overlap with psychology in these areas. In the case of education topics, use the education databases. For marketing, PR, and organizational communication topics, also check out business databases, such as Business Source Complete and Business Source Premier. Finding sources is not just about reaching a certain number of articles or sources, but about using search strategies to be sure we have the best, most useful and on-topic sources available. Therefore, using databases that cover research relevant to our specific topic should help us find the best sources for our specific research topic.

Your topic should tell you what databases would be appropriate: business, psychology, education, religion, etc. If you're really in a bind and can't find sources, there are more general database search engines, such as Academic Search Complete and options to search multiple databases within EBSCO. This broad search takes a lot longer though, and will return mixed, often off-topic results. With a well-developed, specific search phrase, you may find articles using a general search that will be useful to you.

Choosing and keeping track of articles. Clearly, searching for research can be a difficult task, and is not something that can be done quickly. Finding *relevant, inter-related* articles up front is going to make the rest of your project easier. So, it is worth the investment of time to search the literature using a variety of strategies. While you're searching the literature, keep track of the databases you used, the search phrases you used, and the articles you've found that sound interesting. That way, if you find that you need to do more searches, you will know where you have already looked so you won't be doing to same searches over again. You also should be keeping track of relevant articles while you are searching.

Helpful Hint

Don't lose your work! Create an account in the research database if possible, save your search phrases, and save the article records that you find interesting. If you cannot create an account, regularly email records to yourself, take screen shots of useful sources, or copy and paste record details into a file saved to your desktop, so if your Internet connection times out, your work will be saved.

© Odua Images, 2014. Shutterstock, Inc.

Every search engine will be somewhat different in how the information is displayed, but this is the information you can expect to find. When you click on the hyperlinked information in the citation, it will take you to a page that contains detailed information about the article. This page has a lot of useful information:

- Authors' names
- Source title, year, and volume number
- Subject terms you can use to find similar articles
- An abstract, or brief summary of the article contents

ERIC

| Collection | Thesaurus |
| Politic* and (youth OR age OR adole: |

Advanced
Search Tips

Notes
FAQ
Contact Us

☐ Peer reviewed only   ☐ Full text available on ERIC

Back to results

Attitudes toward Political Engagement and Willingness to Participate in Politics: Trajectories throughout Adolescence

Eckstein, Katharina; Noack, Peter; Gniewosz, Burkhard

Journal of Adolescence, v35 n3 p485-495 Jun 2012

Drawing on data from a longitudinal cohort-sequential project, the present study examined developmental trajectories of adolescents' attitudes toward political engagement and their willingness to participate in politics from grade 7 to 11 while accounting for the influence of school track and gender. Moreover, stabilities on the dependent variables were assessed. The results revealed differential trajectories regarding adolescents' educational level. Increases were mainly shown for students attending the college-bound school track. Generally, both orientations toward political behaviors were shown to become more stable throughout the adolescent years. Together, the findings confirmed adolescence to be a crucial period in life concerning the emergence, consolidation, and development of political points of view. (Contains 4 tables and 2 figures.)

Descriptors: Adolescents, Longitudinal Studies, Citizen Participation, Politics, Political Attitudes, Educational Attainment, Gender Differences, Higher Education, Academic Aspiration

Elsevier. 6277 Sea Harbor Drive, Orlando, FL 32887-4800. Tel: 877-839-7126; Tel: 407-345-4020; Fax: 407-363-1354; e-mail: usjcs@elsevier.com; Web site: http://www.elsevier.com

☐ Peer reviewed
☐ Direct link

ERIC Number: EJ967267
Record Type: Journal
Publication Date: 2012-Jun
Pages: 11
Abstractor: As Provided
Reference Count: 0
ISBN: N/A
ISSN: ISSN-0140-1971

The abstract is a brief summary of the article that can help you determine whether the source is likely to be useful to you. It should briefly describe the concepts / theory, method, and results. Store the records for the high quality sources that sound most interesting and relevant to your project.

In addition to the article record and abstract, you also have a list of key terms for the article, or *subject headings / descriptors*, listed in this record. You can choose one of those subject headings to do an entirely new search. This can be useful if you're having trouble finding articles, or if the articles you're finding aren't focused enough or aren't sufficiently interrelated.

Finally, if you find this article to be particularly interesting or relevant to your research purpose, you may want to look at their *cited references*. Their references may contain articles that you would find interesting. By looking at their references while you're still in the database, you can look up any articles in their reference list that sound interesting. For example, in the reference list for one of the returned results, I found this article:

Delli Carpini M. X. "Gen.com: Youth, civic engagement, and the new information environment." Political Communication. v. 17 p. 341–349. 2000

This sounds like it might be useful to our paper. If we're in the database already, we can look it up and store that record for later too.

2. Use Your Library to Find Print Sources

You will typically need to use your library to access published academic research articles, either full text online or in print. Relatively few peer reviewed journal articles are available free online. Your library will also have printed academic journals that you can read there or photocopy, access to electronic copies of many academic journal articles, and both print and electronic copies of newspapers and magazines. When you use an open source search engine such as ERIC or Google Scholar, you will need to go to your library's website to determine whether your library provides access to those sources. If your library does not have access to a particular source in print or online format, their circulation desk may be able to help you order a copy of the source.

Other types of print sources can often be searched for through your library, just as you would search for academic journal articles. General databases like Academic Search Complete can be helpful when finding any type of printed material that your library may have. Most information can be accessed electronically, but you may have to check out hard copies of certain materials from the library itself.

LexisNexis. One database that can be very helpful when searching newspapers, magazines, or legal documents is LexisNexis. LexisNexis operates in the same way as the EBSCO and ERIC databases do, in that you use keywords and search terms to find information. You can narrow your search to just newspapers, or expand it to all worldwide publications. You can also choose to search one particular print source. LexisNexis is helpful for topics that look into current trends or specific events. You can search for and read news reports relevant to people and events to gain insight into the historical background, context, major developments, and people's reactions to events as they occurred. You can also look up specific court cases from state and federal courts. That being said, Lexis-Nexis is not a source for academic literature.

Books. Libraries use catalogs to organize their books, and most use the Library of Congress (LoC) cataloging system. The LoC system organizes books by subject headings then by subtopics within each subject. There are 21 "main classes" of texts in the LoC system: (http://www.loc.gov/catdir/cpso/lcco/):

Library of Congress
Classification Outline

- A - General Works
- B - Philosophy, Psychology, Religion
- C - Auxiliary Sciences of History
- D - World History
- E and F - History of the Americas
- G - Geography, Anthropology, Recreation
- H - Social Sciences
- J - Political Science
- K - Law
- L - Education
- M - Music
- N - Fine Arts
- P - Language and Literature
- Q - Science
- R - Medicine
- S - Agriculture
- T - Technology
- U - Military Science
- V - Naval Science
- Z - Bibliography

Within each of these main classes, there are subtopics for further classification. So, under the main class H, there are subclasses such as Subclass HQ, which includes subjects such as marriage, family, and sexuality. So, if I'm interested in looking for books on relationships, then the H.HQ section in the library is a good place for me to look.

In today's e-society, very few people actually go to the library and look through the stacks anymore. We search for books online much the same way we use search engines and academic databases. Being familiar with the LoC classification system can make searching for library materials, even online, much easier because you will know what subject headings to be looking for in your catalog search.

Most university libraries have two online search options for finding books: the first is to search the library's holdings, the second is to search the holdings of a consortium of libraries from which you can "borrow" books. The resources at any given library are determined by the size of the school, the size of the program, the funding that the library receives, and how the state handles library resources.

Many states offer a single catalog search that allows you to search the catalogs of all participating libraries. This is referred to as a "**shared catalog**," and it is becoming more common for universities to join a consortium of libraries within their respective states to share library holdings. For example, Ohio has Ohio-Link. This database allows both professors and students the ability to search the library holdings of all participating Ohio libraries. If we find something through OhioLink that we need but our own school library doesn't own, we can request it and have it lent to us from another library. This has been an excellent tool for those of us at smaller schools, as we can find and borrow many books that we would not have had access to before catalog sharing became popular.

Beyond your library, you can use more general searches to find books, but you may not be able to access these books through interlibrary loan or as online fulltext documents:

- Worldcat offers a searchable online catalog of titles from participating libraries around the world: http://www.worldcat.org/

Worldcat

- The Library of Congress Online Catalog is a searchable catalog of the LoC holdings: http://catalog.loc.gov/

Library of Congress Online Catalog

One option, if you find a book through Worldcat or the LoC that is not available for loan, is to search via Google to see if it is available via Google Books. In the next section, we discuss some strategies for conducting academic research using popular search engines.

3. Search the Internet

Web search engines: Google, Yahoo!, Bing, Dogpile, and Ask. Search engines are becoming increasingly complex and specialized. However, we rarely venture beyond the search engine homepage to explore the many options that can help us search the Internet. The same Boolean operators that we can use to search academic databases can also be used to search via search engines.

For example, Google offers Scholar, News, and Book search options, so that you can limit the search field to more credible sources or particular types of online content when you search. Bing and Yahoo! also offer a News search. So, if you're interested in books on interpersonal relationships, you can use the Google Book search and / or the Google Scholar search, using the same types of phrases used to search the academic literature.

Check out some of the options available via Google here: http://www.google.com/intl/en/about/products/

Though it can be very helpful to use a search engine to find academic sources, particularly a search engine like Google Scholar, we do have a few words of warning:

- Using Google Scholar *is not the same* as going into an academic database to search peer reviewed publications.
  - o It is not a subject-specific database, so you may get results from many different disciplines.
  - o Full text and / or full bibliographic information may not be available for all of the returned articles. To retrieve full-text copies of articles, you will likely still need to go to your library website and search for the article, ask your librarian, or purchase the article directly from the publisher.
  - o You will likely have hundreds of thousands, if not millions, of items returned using this general Google Scholar search:

- Some of the Google Scholar options are similar to the options in academic databases and can help you limit the number of articles returned and how they are ordered:
  - You can set a date range and limit your results to academic publications.
  - You can arrange results by relevance or in chronological order.
  - You can choose whether your search includes searching through articles' citations or not.
  - You can click on "cited by" or "related articles" for each article listed, and this can lead you to other possible sources for your paper, including other research articles and books. There is also a link to the full text, if it is available online.

Web directories. Moving on from general web searches to more narrow online resources, web directories can also help you find websites that would be useful to you while researching. Think of web directories as an "index" of websites, much like the Library of Congress classification system indexes books. Yahoo!, for example, has a directory feature (http://dir. yahoo.com/). You select the category you are interested in, then select the area you are researching within that category, and it takes you to a list of websites that provide relevant content.

Yahoo! directories

Specialized search engines. The final option that we will discuss in this unit is using a specialized search engine to find sources.

- **ERIC (The Educational Resources Information Center)**. This government-funded site is an open, searchable database of research articles and other reference materials for use by educators. ERIC has many of the functions of EBSCO, but the database of articles is more focused and restricted compared to more general search engines. That being said, ERIC offers more full-text options compared to open source search engines, like Google. ERIC can be accessed here: http://www.eric.ed.gov/

ERIC database

- **Scopus**. Scopus is only available to subscribers, but it functions much like EBSCO and ERIC. It searches academic publications and can be used to track citations. Scopus offers a variety of tools to help you visualize research and search results, and claims to be the largest database of academic research available. You can purchase access to Scopus here: http://www.scopus.com/home.url

Scopus database

- **The Web of Science**. Also a subscription service, WoS offers a citation index and access to academic publication and conference proceedings. You can get more information about the WoS here: http://thomsonreuters .com/web-of-science/

Web of Science
Core Collection

In all, to conduct a search for sources, you have many options available to you. Regardless of the types of sources you are looking for or are required to have for your project, we have outlined the following steps to find sources.

In summary, to find sources, you:

1. Set and follow standards for the *quality* and *relevance* of sources you need to answer your problem question.
2. Identify the *types* of sources you need: academic research articles, books, websites, or other sources.
3. Use specific search strategies to create a simple, accurate *search phrase*, then modify your search phrase as needed.
4. Access *academic databases* or other specialized searches to find academic research articles.
5. Access *library catalogs* to find subject headings and relevant books.

6. Access *general search engines* or *web directories* to find related websites.
7. Keep track of sources that you find, including the database / website, search phrase used, and source details.

REFERENCES

Kerlinger, F. N., & Lee, H. B. (2000). *Foundations of behavioral research* (4th ed.). New York: Harcourt.

University of Toledo Libraries. (2013, September 13). Types of literature reviews. Retrieved from http://libguides.utoledo.edu/content.php?pid=285708&sid=2351630

ACTIVITIES

1. How do they compare?

Choose a brief search phrase that is relevant to your problem question. Do the following, and record *how many results* you get back with each search tool and the *quality* of the results you got using each search option:

- Write a simple, accurate search phrase related to your topic and specific concepts
- Use an academic database search, such as EBSCO's "Communication & Mass Media Complete"
- Use your library's catalog search
- Use Yahoo.com for a general web search
- Use Google Scholar

Which gave you the most results? Did any offer too many or too few results compared to the others? How much overlap did you see in the search results? Which had the best quality results in terms of dates, publication, and author credibility?

2. Recommended Assignment: Source List

Develop a list of credible, interrelated sources that fit your topic and seem to relate to the question you are attempting to answer.

1. Keep track of where you searched and what search phrases you used.
2. Your records for each source should include all of the relevant information for your source: author(s), year, title, abstract / summary, URL, and how you found it.
3. Organize the sources by type (books, websites, and journal articles).
4. Then, within each type of source, list each article type by relevance and credibility, from most to least useful.

You can use this worksheet:

Part 1:   Source List Worksheet

Search Engine / Database:	Complete Search Phrases I Used:
1.	
2.	

Part 2:   Sources for Use Ranked by Relevance

Source Info:	Books	Websites	Journals
Author: Year: Title: How I found it:			

EXAMPLE COMPLETED STEP 2

Part 1:   Search Engines and Phrases

Search Engine / Database:	Complete Search Phrases I Used:
Google	Age AND "political participation"
ERIC	politic* AND (age OR youth OR adolescent)
EBSCO	politic* AND (age OR youth OR adolescent)

Part 2: Sources for Use Ranked by Relevance

	Books	Websites	Journals
Author:	Utter, G. H. (2011).	Smith, A. et al. (2009).	Lee, N., Shah, D. V., & McLeod, J. M. (2013).
Year:			
Title:	Youth and Political Participation: A Reference Handbook.	The demographics of offline and online political participation.	Processes of political socialization: A communication mediation approach to youth civic engagement. *Communication Research, 40*(5), 669–697. EBSCO
How I found it:	Google Books	Pew Internet. Google	
Author:	Zukin, C. (2006).	Smith, A. (2013).	Holt, K., Shehata, A., Strömbäck, J., & Ljungberg, E. (2013)
Title:	A New Engagement? Political Participation, Civic Life, and the Changing American Citizen. Google.	Civic engagement in the digital age.	Age and the effects of news media attention and social media use on political interest and participation: Do social media function as leveller? *European Journal of Communication, 28*(1), 19–34. EBSCO
How I found it:		Pew Internet. Google	
Author:		Xi	Jenkins, H., & Carpentier, N. (2013).
Year:		2013	
Title:		Online political activism grows, but "slacktivism" remains. PBS MediaShift.	Theorizing participatory intensities: A conversation about participation and politics. *Convergence: The Journal of Research into New Media Technologies, 19*(3), 265–286. EBSCO
How I found it:		Google	
Author:			Hanlong Fu, Yi Mou, Miller, M. J., & Jalette, G. (2011).
Title:			Reconsidering political cynicism and political involvement: A test of antecedents. *American Communication Journal, 13*(2), 44–61. EBSCO

Tryon, C.
(2008).
Pop politics: Online parody videos, iontertextuality, and political participation.
Popular Communication, 6(4), 209–213.
EBSCO

Pasek, J., Kenski, K., Romer, D., & Jamieson, K. H.
(2006).
America's youth and community engagement: How use of mass media Is related to civic activity and political awareness in 14- to 22-year-olds.
Communication Research, 33(3), 115–135.
EBSCO

Coleman, S.
(1999).
The new media and democratic politics. *New Media & Society, 1*(1), 67–74.
EBSCO

STEP 3

The Third Step in Your Investigation: Look Closely at the Evidence

Good detectives do not skim, scroll through, or gloss over evidence. Rather, they look closely at the details, take snapshots and careful notes, and keep comprehensive files on their investigations. You too will need to look very closely at the evidence you've collected in your investigation and take notes on the sources you've collected. In this chapter, we offer some suggestions for how to read and take notes on different types of source content that you may be citing for your literature review.

One important thing to keep in mind as you start the process of reading and taking notes is that not all information in the sources you found will be equally relevant to your own literature review. You may not use some of your sources, and you may, after reading, find more sources that are useful to you. As you read and take notes, focus on those sources that are most relevant to your paper, be open to finding new leads, and focus your note taking on the *parts* of sources that are relevant to your paper.

THIS CHAPTER COVERS:

A. How to Read Academic Sources
   1. Reading Books: What to Look For
      a. Review the Table of Contents to Find Main Points/Topics
      b. Use the Index to Find Concepts and Authors in the Text
      c. Look at Who They Cited
   2. Reading Academic Research Articles and Book Chapters that Report Research Studies: What to Look For
      a. Parts of an Academic Research Article
      b. Reading the Literature Review
      c. Reading the Method Section
      d. Reading the Results Section
      e. Reading the Discussion Section
B. Writing an Annotation
   1. Summarizing and Paraphrasing
   2. Writing a Reference in APA Style
      a. Journal Articles
      b. Chapters in Edited Books
      c. Books
      d. Websites
C. Examples

Once you've found sources, your focus becomes synopsizing, or summarizing, those sources. This is, for most students, the most difficult and time-consuming part of their first academic writing project. Even for seasoned writers and researchers, it can be difficult to read and pick up on some of the jargon and technical details in academic writing. The goal of critically reading and taking notes is to take a substantial collection of research, and compress it into a more manageable form. So, we take 20+ page academic journal articles, academic books, and websites and write brief summaries of those sources. Also, this gives us an opportunity to put together a tentative reference list in APA style. To put together an annotation, which is the one note-taking strategy we cover in this chapter, you need to understand what type of sources you have, what information from that source is relevant and necessary to use, how to paraphrase, and how to write a reference in APA style. We'll begin by addressing the fundamentals of reading academic research, then review types of research to be aware of, and finally overview each part of the article and what you should look for to include in your annotations.

A. How to Read Academic Sources

1. Reading Books: What to Look For

Review the table of contents to find main points/topics. Books are organized into chapters, and chances are that not every chapter is going to be equally useful and relevant to your paper. The detailed table of contents offered in most academic books will give you a thorough overview of the content covered in the book. Chances are, you will only need one or two chapters of the book, and so you can find the chapters you need to read and take notes on by looking at the detailed table of contents. If no detailed table of contents is offered, reading the introductory section of each chapter should give you enough information to choose which chapters are most relevant to your topic.

Once you have chosen which chapters you will need from the book, you can create an outline of the chapter to guide your note taking. In the first couple of paragraphs, there should be a thesis and preview of the chapter. Then the chapter should, point-by-point, thoroughly cover that topic. Knowing the basics of good writing style will help you read and outline a chapter:

- The first paragraphs should have a thesis, or main idea for the entire chapter. Make a note of this. This should tell you on which part of the chapter to focus.
- There should be headings throughout the chapter that clearly label each main point. Make note of these. Closely read and take notes on the parts of the chapter that are relevant to your problem question.

- Each paragraph within each main point should have a thesis statement. These are the key concepts/arguments in each section. Outline the key points in the paragraphs that are most important to your paper.

Use the index to find concepts and authors in the text. Sometimes, we are only using a book to look up definitions, or for a discussion of a very narrow and specific concept that is explained in that book. These details may not be covered in the table of contents, so it would be appropriate to look up the concept we need to read about in the index. Using the index, much like finding sources in academic research databases, requires that we know the exact theory, variable, or concept name. The index will give the name of the concept followed by the page numbers where that concept is referenced in the text. You can go directly to those pages to see if the information is useful.

Many academic books will also have an author index, which lists all of the authors that are cited in the book and the page numbers where those specific authors are cited. If there is a particular researcher whose research you're interested in, you can use the author index to see where their work is referenced in the text, and go there to read more about his or her work.

When you are using an online book, such as a Google Book or a Kindle book, you can search for your key terms throughout the book and go directly to the sections that are most relevant to your research interests. This is particularly useful in textbooks, where a concept may be discussed several times in different contexts, but may not appear in the table of contents or index.

Helpful Hint

When reading through a book, check to see if it is available as a pdf or online book, such as a Google Book. If you can access the text, even a limited preview of the text, use the search feature to find where your key concepts, variables, theory, and/or authors of interest are mentioned in the book. Then you'll know exactly where to look in the print book to find relevant information.

© doomu, 2014. Shutterstock, Inc.

Look at who they cited. In addition to the author index (when there is one), looking at the references that are cited in books can lead you to some very useful sources you otherwise might not have found. For example, communication textbooks will typically cite the seminal, or first and most influential, articles or books on a topic. So, by looking at their list of references, you will get a full citation that you can use to find that seminal piece. You can also look at which authors are cited most frequently, and look up the most-cited authors yourself to read their research. This is done by doing an author search in an academic research database or by Googling the author's name (preferably in Google Scholar).

2. Reading Academic Research Articles and Book Chapters that Report Research Studies: What to Look For

Every piece of research will focus on a small set of concepts or variables. Each author should a) define the variables and concepts in the literature review, b) explain how the variables and concepts may be related or what they expect to find (typically in the form of hypotheses, research questions, or a statement of purpose), c) explain how they measured or assessed those variables or concepts, d) report what they found in regard to those variables or concepts, and e) explain how they contributed to our understanding of human communication in the discussion section.

Therefore, for the concepts and variables relevant to your paper, you should look at how they are defined in the literature review, expected to relate to other variables in the hypotheses, measured or analyzed in the method section, and related to other variables or described in the results section. Because it is each author's unique approach to the variables being studied that we hope to glean from these articles, it is important that we treat them carefully by *never renaming variables*, being true to the author's unique definition of the variables in our notes, and being clear and specific about how they are analyzed and what was found.

It is also unethical to use sources that another person has cited without retrieving and reading those sources. What authors present in the review of literature is their paraphrase of what other people have written in the past. Therefore, we need to go back to the original, primary source before we cite an article.

a. Parts of an Academic Research Article

Academic journal articles are generally critiques, syntheses, or original research. The vast majority of published academic journal articles are original research, though several publications (like *Community Theory* and *Communication Yearbook*) tend to publish predominantly syntheses and critiques.

Original research is typically presented in full-length manuscripts or reports. Full-length manuscripts are 25 to 30 pages of text and reports are shorter (15 pages or less). Full-length manuscripts will have a more developed review of literature, but both reports and full-length articles should have a thorough explanation of the study conducted. Regardless of the type of manuscript, papers often have a literature review, method, results, and discussion section and end with a list of references, tables, and/or figures. The quality and depth of these article components varies widely, though. For example, some articles will only briefly talk about a method then go into their analysis.

Shon (2012) offers some suggestions about what to look for in an academic research article:

- Introduction: What did they do?
- Literature review: Is this a critique, summary, or identifying and filling gaps in existing research?
- Results: What were the key findings?
- Discussion: What was consistent and inconsistent with previous research? What did these authors do and what should be done next?

We expand on each of these elements of academic writing in the following sections and offer suggestions for what to look for in communication studies research articles in particular.

b. Reading the Literature Review

The literature review is where students new to academic research tend to focus their attention. Though this is not always the *most* important part of the manuscript, it is an essential component so that we understand the justification, concepts, and hypotheses or research questions in the study. The literature review is a discussion of the previously conducted research related to the topic of the paper. Depending on the type of literature review, the authors may compare and contrast, offer a chronology, critique, apply, or argue for a new theory.

Let's look at each of these approaches. In the **compare and contrast approach**, authors look at different areas of study or different theories and explain the ways that they overlap and the ways that they are different. This is typically done to set up a study that integrates assumptions from two or more theories. In the **chronological approach**, researchers trace the history of a concept or theory over time, point out key developments and turning points in a theory's history, and point to directions for future research. In a **critique**, the main points of the literature review typically focus on what has been done in the past and what remains unknown or is unclear. **Application reviews**, which are typically done for case studies, focus on arguing for why a set of concepts or a theory relate to the specific person or event being studied. Lastly, some literature reviews are a direct argument for a **new theory** that is built by referencing existing research. Understanding the type of literature review you are reading should help you take notes and direct your attention to the most important points in the review. We know, for example, if it is a compare/contrast literature review, that we should note the key similarities and differences between the items being compared. If it is a historical review, we should make note of the key turning points that the authors discuss.

Regardless of the type of literature review, if the article is reporting a full study, there is usually some discussion of conclusions, omissions, inconsistencies,

STEP 3

ambiguities, or inaccuracies in the existing literature that suggest the need for the present study. This is done to frame and *justify* the present study.

Another important part of all well-written literature reviews is conceptualization of concepts and variables. They also use existing literature to define, in their own way, the variables being researched. This process is called **conceptualization**. Conceptual definitions of concepts are typically based on the synthesis of previous studies.

Based on the discussion and critique of existing research, most researchers will propose hypotheses and/or research questions that address the variables that they have discussed in the literature review. **Hypotheses** *are assumptions* and **research questions** *are inquiries*, based on the literature reviewed, about how specific variables will be *related to each other*.

Hypotheses, particularly for quantitative studies, can be tricky to read and interpret for people who are new to research. Here are a few quick reminders about the language you may encounter in hypotheses and some research questions:

- Variables may be **positively related**, or, put another way, when one variable goes up the other variable goes up.
- Variables may also be **negatively related**, or, when one goes up, the other goes down. For example, as education goes up, income goes up (a positive relationship). As education goes up, other problems associated with sociodemographics go down (a negative relationship).
- Researchers often use a **regression** to determine how a set of predictor variables are related to an outcome variable. So we may see how a combination of variables, like parents' education and family income, *predict* children's educational attainment.
- Variables may also increase or decrease across different conditions or from one group to the next, which is referred to as a **mean difference**. For example, income is highest among people who have earned graduate degrees and lowest among groups without a high school diploma (a mean difference in income between two groups).
- Sometimes, we are trying to *describe* or discover a variable or concept. For example, we may ask a research question about how parents communicate with their children about higher education. In these types of studies, researchers will discover and explain themes, trends, and/or categories that emerge from the data.

Your goal for the literature review, then, should be to find the important variables, concepts, and theories; identify how the researcher defines (or conceptualizes) those variables and concepts; and identify how the researcher expects variables to be related to each other (hypotheses/research questions/purpose).

c. Reading the Method Section

If the article is a full study, the next section of a published article will typically be the method section. After the researcher proposes hypotheses or research

Helpful Hints for Reading Literature Reviews

© doomu, 2014. Shutterstock, Inc.

- Look at the headings used throughout the literature review to ascertain the author's approach to the topic (comparison, historical, critical, application, etc.) and their main ideas and key concepts. Each section is typically a critique, turning point, variable, concept, or collection of related variables and concepts.

- Hypotheses are usually labeled (i.e., H1, H2, etc.); research questions are also typically labeled (RQ1, RQ2, etc.). If they aren't labeled, look closely at the end of each major section of the paper, or the end of the literature review, for statements such as "We expect to find that…" or "We propose that…" or "Our goal is to…"

questions, they are going to explain how they tested that hypothesis or explored those questions. Before being able to effectively discuss research in our own literature review, we need to understand the types of research. We consider the approach to research (quantitative, qualitative, or critical), the method used (deductive, inductive, or case study), and the data collection technique (sample and method of data collection). This section will address these types of research so that you will recognize them when you are reading the articles for your literature review.

Research approaches and operationalization. Generally, communication research is quantitative, qualitative, or critical. You will likely notice when you're reading studies for your research project that the majority of the studies you read will be in one of those areas. For example, if you decide to conduct your first research project on agenda-setting theory, you will find that most of the research on that theory is quantitative: researchers use surveys, polls, and content analysis to track changes in media coverage and people's opinions. On the other hand, if you're looking at relationship maintenance strategies, you may find studies that are more qualitative, involving interviews with couples to explore different ways that people maintain their relationships, and some studies that are quantitative and use survey measures of strategies. On the other hand, if you're interested in image repair, you will likely find that a lot of research is critical in that it evaluates different people's and organizations' use of different image repair strategies.

Quantitative research uses statistical analysis of variables' relationships or frequencies and involves the use of surveys with scales (like personality scales, frequencies of communication behaviors, etc.), content analysis and coding (counting elements in message content), and experiments (where something is manipulated to measure its effects). Quantitative studies are done to *predict* outcomes and *explain* how/if variables are related to each other. Quantitative studies involve clear operationalization of variables. **Operationalization** is how a particular variable is measured or analyzed.

Qualitative research, on the other hand, *describes* variables like relationship development, conflict strategies, and personal experiences during media use, etc. to help us understand categories, themes, typologies, or groupings of individual dispositions, relationships, experiences, or communication tactics.

Finally, **critical research** is evaluative. It critiques the use of communication tactics by looking for specific strategies (rhetorical tactics) across different contexts to explore how messages are constructed.

Table 3.1   Research Approaches and Operationalization

Quantitative: *Predict* and *Explain* *Relationships Among* Variables	Qualitative: *Describe and Categorize* Variables	Critical: *Evaluate* Content
• Surveys	• Interviews	• Historical Research
• Content Analysis	• Open-ended Surveys	• Application of Lenses to Texts
• Experiments	• Focus Groups	• Criticism of Texts
• Coding Open Responses	• Content Studies	

Helpful Hint

Authors often use a group of variables, called a **typology**. It is important to make note of the definitions of each part of the typology. For example, a researcher may study "personality." But, they are going to look at specific personality traits, like "the Big 5." Be sure to note the definition of *each component of the typology*. Another researcher may also look at personality, but look at argumentativeness and aggression, so making note of these details can help us see how these articles fit together later in the process of writing our papers.

© doomu, 2014. Shutterstock, Inc.

Types of Methods in Communication. There are three types of studies conducted in communication: deductive, inductive, and case studies. **Deductive**

approaches are typically empirical, and use quantitative analysis to test a theory or model. **Inductive approaches** are qualitative and are used to develop a theory that emerges from data. Lastly, **case studies** have elements of deductive and inductive methods, as they typically involve a theory-centered approach to analyzing a person or communication event, but they also have elements of inductive analysis as these types of studies are typically qualitative or critical. Part of being able to read and interpret the method section of an academic research paper is recognizing the type of method the authors are using.

Deductive theory or model tests are empirical studies. Arguably, a significant proportion of communication research that is published in scholarly journals is research that tests, critiques, or extends a communication theory or develops and tests models of the communication process. *Deductive theory tests are carefully designed studies that test or apply one or more variables, concepts, or assumptions of a theory or model.* Theories and communication models have multiple assumptions about how variables are related. These types of research are typically empirical or quantitative studies that employ statistical analysis to test and confirm or disconfirm assumptions. These studies are *deductive because they begin with a theory or research-based hypotheses*, then employ a method to test relationships, then reach conclusions about the relationships among variables based on their findings.

That being said, research that tests or extends existing theories takes numerous forms: it may be survey, experimental, observational, or content analytic. Theory research is unique, however, because it is guided by the concepts from the theory it is applying. Tests of models are typically quantitative, because they involve testing the causal assumptions of a model.

When reading this type of study, make note of the *operationalizations* in the method section, or how researchers plan to measure their variables. What did they measure or manipulate? How did they measure or manipulate each variable?

Inductive theory development is grounded. When there is no existing theory to explain a communication phenomenon, sometimes researchers will use a grounded approach to see if a theory emerges from their data. This is typically done qualitatively, by asking open questions, looking for themes, trends, and categories in responses, and developing a theory based on what emerges from the data. *This method is inductive because the theory is developed after data collection.* When reading the method section for this type of study, look closely at the procedures that were used to reach conclusions. What did they examine? How did they analyze the data?

Case studies. A case study is typically an in-depth look at a specific person, organization, event, or situation to explain the communication that occurred and gain insight into communication processes and practices. Case studies are common in critical and qualitative research, as they are often content-based studies that explain what happened (i.e., researchers ask "what happened here?") and also evaluative (i.e., researchers ask "what could have been done better?"). When looking at the methods employed in a case study, ask pointed questions about the case and approach: What did they look at to reach their conclusions? What advice can be gleaned from these findings? What is unique and important about this case?

Helpful Hint

Have a methods book handy when you read through the method and results section of academic research studies. Methods books typically have a glossary, so you can use the glossary to find definitions of terms that you read in the articles that you may not fully understand. There are some open-access textbooks available online, such as Bhattacherjee's (2012) Social Science Research: Principles, Methods, and Practices (http://scholarcommons.usf.edu/oa_textbooks/3/).

© Odua Images, 2014. Shutterstock, Inc.

Types of Data in Communication Studies. Every type of research will have some sort of data that is used to reach conclusions about communication phenomena. As you read through the method section, it is important to consider the type of data you are reading about, as this will help you understand the findings of the study and also serve as something you can use to critique, or evaluate, the quality of the study. *Data is what the researchers analyze, and it can be anything that is textual, verbal, visual, or behavioral.* We can observe human behavior, analyze responses to questions, or look at different types of mediated content.

Regardless of the type of data, we have to read critically to understand the sampling method that was used to collect or acquire that data. *Sampling is choosing who, or what, we look at from within a population.* Typically, we simply cannot collect data from everyone or everything in the group that we are interested in researching. Therefore, we select a sample from the group we're looking at, and we analyze data collected from that sample. Different sampling methods lead to different types of problems with **generalizing**, or making sweeping conclusions, about findings. Only **random samples**, or samples that are randomly drawn from the entire population, are considered generalizable. And even then, generalizability depends on the size of the sample. Some other types of sampling include:

- **Convenience samples** are samples that we use because they are easily available to us. For example, we often use college students for research participants because it is convenient.
- **Purposive sampling** is when we select what we analyze based on specific criteria relevant to our study. For example, there may just be one group of people I'm interested in analyzing, so I would purposively sample people in that group.
- **Snowball sampling** is when we select a group, then use that group to refer us to or collect data from other people. So, for example, I may ask someone relevant to my research design to distribute surveys to people in their social or professional group.
- **Stratified sampling** is when we have a pattern to choosing who or what we include in our sample, such as choosing even numbered episodes of a TV show, or every 10th person in the phonebook to call.
- **Quota sampling** is when a specific percentage, or quota, is set for your sample. For example, I may want 50% men and 50% women in my sample, so I would set a quota based on gender.

As a critical consumer of information, being aware of the sampling method used in the study you are reading will help you understand the generalizability of the results you read. The sampling method that is appropriate for any given study depends on the type of study being conducted. There are many different ways to collect and analyze data, and we will focus on a few of the most common approaches in communication research here.

Content studies. Content studies are common in rhetorical theory research, cultural studies, media research, and political communication research. Content studies include looking for textual, visual, or production elements in print, audio, televised, or computer-mediated messages. Academics and practitioners may be interested, for example, in the gender roles depicted in cartoons. They would define what they mean by "gender roles," then choose a series of cartoons to watch to find instances that meet that definition. For example, Chu and McIntyre (1995) looked at the depiction of gender role stereotypes in cartoon characters and found that male characters demonstrated stereotypical male tendencies and female characters had more stereotypically feminine behaviors. This can be done *quantitatively* by counting instances. It may also be done *qualitatively* by looking for trends in media content. Lastly, it may be done *critically* by closely evaluating media content or looking for evidence of biased gender roles.

Survey studies. Survey studies are conducted face-to-face, using paper and pencil, or online. They may involve open questions and closed questions (such as Likert items, yes/no questions, etc.). They are used to collect many different types of information, such as having people self-report their attitudes, feelings, perceptions, beliefs, values, and behaviors. Surveys allow us to observe trends when they are collected over time, and they help us better understand large groups of people.

Research on trends is particularly popular in mass media research. People research the dissemination of new technology, use of existing technology, changes/fluctuations in audience preferences, and changes in media content. We also do a lot of research on trends in opinion and sociodemographics. *Trend studies tend to be large-scale studies that look for substantial, systematic changes in a particular variable over time by conducting the same survey with a different sample over and over again.* Some common types of trend studies are conducted on social variables (marriage and divorce rates, birth rates, socio-economic status, etc.), consumer variables (spending habits and consumer confidence), employment variables (fluctuation in employment rates, types of jobs, and pay), and variables related to public opinion (support for issues, politicians, etc.).

We can also conduct **panel surveys**, *which survey a specific sample of people over time to see how they change.* These types of studies give us more causal information compared to trend surveys, because we can observe changes in people and look at variables that might explain why some people on our panel changed and why others may not have changed.

Surveys can also help us understand people: who they are, what they think, and what they do. This is typically done using a **cross-section survey**, *or a single-shot survey that captures information just once.* These types of surveys are used to explore the motivations, personality, attitudes, beliefs, values, behaviors, demographics, and other characteristics of an audience or group of people at a single point in time.

Surveys can be a useful tool for collecting a lot of information about a lot of people. We have many well-established scale measures that we use in survey research in communication that help us develop reliable and valid surveys. That being said, surveys do have some drawbacks. Surveys rely on self-reported data. Put another way, surveys depend on people to provide accurate, honest responses to sometimes very personal questions. People may try to figure out what the researcher wants to find, may intentionally be dishonest, or may even not be able to answer questions accurately. Consider, for example, asking people something simple, like "how many hours did you spend online yesterday?" Chances are, they can give you an estimate. But if they have a smartphone, a laptop, a Roku box, and an internet TV, they probably can't remember every time they checked their email, social networks, watched a streaming video, or searched for something on the web. So, responses to questions like that will probably not reflect people's actual behavior. As you go through survey studies, think critically about the questions that researchers asked: Would people want to answer those questions? Are the questions too direct or too indirect? Are people being asked to report or describe things that they may not be able to accurately report or describe?

Experiments. Experiments are typically done in a lab, or a controlled setting, but they are also sometimes conducted online. In an experiment, participants are divided into two or more groups. One group is exposed to some kind of experimental manipulation that is planned by the researcher in advance, and the other groups may get a different kind of manipulation or no manipulation at all (called a **control group**). We do experiments to see how changing one or two specific variables in the communication situation may change specific dependent variables. Experiments are typically better for establishing **causality**—or being able to say that one variable causes another to change—but they are still limited in their generalizability much like non-random survey samples. Experiments typically have a very small, often non-random samples of participants. And there are also issues with **ecological validity**, or the fact that experiments take place in an artificial environment. The mere act of putting people in an artificial setting can affect experimental results. So, sometimes, experimental results may demonstrate causality, but not accurately reflect how people react and respond in real life. As a critical consumer of this type of research, pay close attention to how the researchers developed and executed their manipulation and the type of people who participated in the experiment and ask yourself: "Do the results likely reflect how people really think, feel, and behave?"

Focus Groups. Focus groups are common in applied communication research and certain types of exploratory studies. Focus groups are small groups, facilitated by the researcher who asks open questions, letting people build on each other's responses, and generally encourages an open dialogue about something relevant to their research purpose. The data from focus groups can be rich and insightful, and the research often uses this method to discover variables, perspectives on a topic, or trends in people's thoughts, feelings, or behaviors. On the other hand, the sample size for focus groups tends to be small, even when multiple focus groups are conducted for a single study. Additionally, focus groups are susceptible to researcher bias and to normative effects within the group itself. Sometimes people keep their opinions to themselves when there seems to be consensus in a group. Sometimes the researcher's own behavior can make people more or less comfortable expressing themselves in this kind of setting. Are these the types of questions people would typically be comfortable answering in a group?

Interviews. Interviews are a research method that is similar to the focus group, only they are conducted one-on-one rather than in a group setting. Interview research can be a great way to get very detailed insight into a person's experiences, interpretations, and beliefs. They are also sometimes a good way to get people to open up about personal details. That being said, interviews also suffer from some of the potential problems of focus groups: the sample used tends to be small and non-random and sometimes it's difficult for people to open up and be honest with a stranger—particularly a researcher—in a one-on-one context.

Observation. Rather than asking people to describe their behavior in a survey, focus group, or interview, researchers can observe people's behavior online or out in the "real world" to collect data. Observing people is becoming much easier with advancements in spyware, open datasets made available by websites, and other unobtrusive methods of watching what people do. These observations can give us a tremendous amount of insight into what people do, and how different types of people behave differently in particular settings. That being said, because for ethical reasons we usually have to make people aware that they are being observed before using any data collected, the mere act of observing people often changes their behavior. Think about it this way, when you lived with your parents, did you act differently when they were home versus when you were home alone? Chances are you did—and still do—act differently when you know that people are watching and taking notes about your behavior. We tend to let our guard down as we become more comfortable, but this can take a long time for people. So, for these types of studies, consider what the researchers were looking for in people's behavior, but also how they observed behavior: Was the researcher present? How many people did they observe? How long did they observe?

So, there are several things for us to consider as we read through the method section, and this should inform our interpretation of the results section. In the methods section, look at:

- The approach: Is it qualitative, quantitative, or critical?
- The method: Is it deductive, inductive, or a case study?
- The sampling method: Is it random or nonrandom?
- The data collected: Is it from the media, websites, surveys, experiments, focus groups, interviews, or observations?

Consider how each of these decisions made by the researchers might impact the results of the study.

d. Reading the Results Section

Students all too often skip reading the results, particularly for quantitative studies. The numbers, statistical symbols, and jargon-laden explanations of findings can be confusing. For example, an ICA conference paper available through a communication database contains the following:

RQ2a asked if there are any differences in self-disclosure between FtF and CMC contexts. Results of one-way repeated-measures ANOVA indicated that people disclose significantly more in FtF settings (M = 29.84, SD = 4.13) than in CMC context (M = 28.09, SD = 4.63), F (1/346) = 64.29, p < .001, eta^2 = .16 (Wang & Anderson, 2007, p. 18).

Here, the authors are reporting the results of a statistical analysis that was used to test a research question. If we omit the statistical information and numbers from the paragraph and note that CMC and FtF are explained earlier in the text, though, the results they're reporting make perfect sense:

RQ2a asked if there are any differences in self-disclosure between [face-to-face] and [computer-mediated communication] contexts. Results...indicated that people disclose significantly more in [face-to-face] settings...than in [computer-mediated communication] context[s] (Wang & Anderson, 2007, p. 18).

Now that we understand what the authors are saying, we can paraphrase their findings by putting it in our own words:

People disclosed more when communicating face-to-face compared to mediated interactions.

Students may wonder why it is important to read the results section when the discussion section includes a review of results. The answer is simple: sometimes, we accentuate certain findings and minimize or gloss over other findings in the discussion section. Therefore, the most complete, unencumbered view of a study's findings is in the results section. In this section, we look to see whether hypotheses were supported or not and how research questions were answered. We determine which variables were related to each other (through prediction, mean differences, etc.) and how they were related (positively, negatively, etc.) and/or summarize the key trends or themes that were identified in the analysis. We also list the key findings.

Terms you should know when reading results sections:

Check out http://stattrek.com/statistics/dictionary.aspx for a dictionary of statistics or http://srmo.sagepub.com/view/the-sage-dictionary-of-social-research-methods/SAGE.xml to subscribe to a dictionary of social scientific research terminology.

Stat Trek Statistics
and Probability
Dictionary

Dictionary of
Statistics and Social
Research Methods

Table 3.2   Terms

Positive Relationship/ Positively Related	As one variable goes up another variable goes up. *Ex.* Education and income are positively related. More educated people tend to make more money.
Negative Relationship / Negatively Related	As one variable goes up, the other variable goes down. *Ex.* Education and debt are negatively related. More educated people tend to carry less debt.
Curvilinear Relationship	One variable peaks at the midpoint of another variable. *Ex.* Rate of pregnancy is curvilinearly related to age: it is low at ages 1 month to 16 years, peaks at 28, and is low again at 40 to 80 years.
Mean Difference	Variable means (or averages) were different between groups. *Ex.* Women score better on nonverbal recognition measures. So, women's mean scores are higher than men's.
Significant/Statistically Significant	The likelihood that the findings are not due to chance. Non-significant results suggest that the variables may not be related; significant results suggest that the variables may be related.
Mediating Variable/ Mediated Relationship	A variable that links one variable to another variable. For example, if A causes B and B causes C, then B is a mediating variable.
Moderating Variable	A variable that affects the relationship between two variables. When A and C both change because of B, then B is a moderating variable.
Validity	The likelihood that researchers are measuring the variable that they intend to measure.
Reliability	The likelihood that the same results can be found over and over again.
Mixed Support	Typically found for a multi-part hypothesis where parts of the hypothesis are supported and other parts of the hypothesis are not supported.
Predictor/Independent Variable	The variable that predicts/determines the other variable(s).
Outcome/Dependent Variable	The variable that is being predicted or explained.
Variance	The amount of variation, or difference, in a variable.
ANOVA	An analysis of variance; it tests whether two or more variables have similar or different means in different groups.
t-Test	An analysis of whether a variable has different means between two groups.
Correlation	An analysis of relationship; it tests whether two variables are positively, negatively, or (for certain correlational analyses) curvilinearly related.
Regression	An analysis of whether a set of independent variables predicts an outcome variable.
Path Model	An analysis of the inter-relationships among independent variables, and how (or if) those variables predict the outcome variable(s).
Structural Equation Model	A test of a causal model, where one set of variables may predict a second set of variables which may, in turn, predict a third set of variables. It may be either exploratory (explores how variables are related) or confirmatory (confirms that variables are related in a particular way).

Table 3.2 Terms (*Continued*)

Factor Analysis	A test of the dimensionality of a measure. It helps researchers see how items in a scale group together statistically.
Rhetorical/Critical Lens	A particular rhetorical perspective which prescribes what the critic is going to look for in the message.
Grounded Theory	Coding data to see what variables, concepts, or themes emerge. The findings that emerge are used to create a theory.
Content Analysis	A method of analyzing communication that involves coding, or counting pre-defined elements in communication.
Pre- and Post-test Design	An experiment where there was a test of the variables, then a treatment or experimental manipulation, then a post-test to see if the variables changed.
Control group	In an experiment, this is the group that is not given the treatment/experimental manipulation so researchers can assess the extent of the effects of the treatment.

e. Reading the Discussion Section

The discussion section puts the results in some context and attempts to explain why these results were found. Results sections typically contain an overview of the study findings with an explanation of why these results were found, an explanation of where this study fits in the larger body of literature on the subject (why it is important), limitations of the study, and directions for future research.

It is useful to read through the discussion to see how the researchers feel their results fit with other people's results. *Note whether the results were the same as, or different from, other, similar studies.* You will need this type of information for your discussion of the research: They may have found an important missing link that other researchers missed, or challenged a long-held assumption in the communication discipline, or linked together variables that have not been addressed in previous research. Take careful notes on why this study is important.

Next, look at their limitations. Every study has limitations: there are often issues with sample size or population, the way questions were asked, or questions that weren't included but should have been. Most authors will discuss the limitations of their studies. Even if they do not, though, you should ask yourself: what about their method likely affected their findings?

B. Writing an Annotation

While you're reading, it is very helpful to take notes to keep track of the content you're reading and also your own reactions, critiques, or questions about that content. One method of taking notes on articles is annotating. **Annotations** are brief summaries that we use to keep track of important content from the sources we plan to use in our research. It typically includes a brief but thorough overview of the source. Taking careful notes on the sources we're citing can help us avoid plagiarism, immerse us in the literature, and help us keep track of which source had what content.

Why Annotate?

Many professors require annotations or annotated reference lists with students' work. Students often wonder why professors require annotations, and there are a couple of reasons we do this. First, it helps your professor check your comprehension of what you have read. The last thing we want is to have misrepresented or misinterpreted information in the literature review you write. Second, it takes hundreds of pages of content and boils it down to a manageable and organized set of notes. This makes writing your paper much easier, since it saves you from having to flip back-and-forth between different sources during the writing process. Third, it helps you avoid "cherry-picking" evidence. Being thorough in your review of the evidence means that you may find articles that support your expectations or refute them. Fourth, it helps immerse you in the research. Rather than skimming through articles, you must read and think critically about them. Lastly, it trains you to look for specific information in the articles you read, so that later on you can read academic research with (relative) ease. Annotating helps us objectively and thoroughly read the evidence before reaching a conclusion.

What an Annotation Is (and Is Not)

Think of annotations as small "book reports" that you write to keep track of your sources. They are detailed notes that *summarize* the key ideas in a source you plan to use for your paper. Before going over what to include in an annotation, let's consider what an annotation *is not*:

- *It is not an abstract.* An **abstract** is a one paragraph summary of what was studied and a few key findings. An abstract can be informative when deciding whether or not to annotate a source, but it does not contain enough information upon which to base arguments in your paper. Relying on abstracts rather than detailed annotations may lead us to misinterpret, misrepresent, or gloss over important details.
- *It is not just a quick, simple note.* An annotation is generally detailed. It can include notes about your reaction to the content, the relevance of the content to your topic, etc., but it should also include a discussion of specific content from the article that led to your reactions.
- *It is not a description, or list, of the content.* Students are often tempted to list the content of the article (e.g., "they discussed three variables, then they did a survey, and they found strong results"). Annotations look at the content and summarize it (e.g., "they measured emotional and informational political attitudes and voting decisions on scales that were administered through surveys. They found that when emotion and information contradicted, people voted based on emotions.").

- *It is not a sentence-by-sentence paraphrase of everything in the source.* Not everything in an article, book, or chapter is relevant to your research question, so not all of it needs to find its way into your annotation. Instead, focus on the most important details in the article relevant to your paper. Typically, the sources they cite, the names of scales and specific statistics, and frequencies and other statistics from the method and results are important to read, but do not need to be in your annotation.
- *It is not a list of quotes from the source.* Some sources do have profound, meaningful quotes. Many do not. If you find a particularly *meaningful* quote, make note of it. But the vast majority of an annotation is a paraphrase of the most important ideas in the source.

1. Summarizing and Paraphrasing

Paraphrasing can be difficult: It involves taking someone else's ideas, condensing them, and putting them into our own words without significantly changing the meaning. For example, consider this excerpt from Kenneth Burke's (1969) *A Rhetoric of Motives*:

> You persuade a man only insofar as you can talk his language by speech, gesture, tonality, order, image, attitude, idea, *identifying* your ways with his. Persuasion by flattery is but a special case of persuasion in general. But flattery can safely serve as our paradigm if we systematically widen its meaning, to see behind it the conditions of identification or consubstantiality in general (p. 55).

This is a very complex, but brilliant explanation of a persuasive tactic, and something worth noting if we are annotating Burke's book. But rather than use the long quote from Burke, we can take it apart to find its meaning, and put it into our own words.

Table 3.3   Paraphrasing

Original wording	Too close to original wording	Paraphrased wording
"You persuade a man only insofar as you can talk his language by speech, gesture, tonality, order, image, attitude, idea, *identifying* your ways with his"	People persuade by identifying, which is using others' language, gesture, tonality, order, image, and attitude or idea.	People have to make themselves seem similar to the people they are trying to influence.
"Persuasion by flattery is but a special case of persuasion in general. But flattery can safely serve as our paradigm if we systematically widen its meaning, to see behind it the conditions of identification or consubstantiality in general"	Identification is flattery if we systematically widen its meaning, to see behind it the many types of identification and consubstantiality that occur.	Identification is a form of flattery.

Read more about Burke's rhetoric here: http://books.google. com/books/about/A_Rhetoric_of_Motives.html?id=y4o7549eC8C

Burke's rhetoric

Common Mistake

When writing about academic research, or using any source content, be careful not to commit plagiarism.

Common forms of plagiarism include:

© Thomas Bethge, 2014. Shutterstock, Inc.

- Failing to use quotation marks around phrases or other direct quotes from the source.

- Failing to correctly or clearly attribute paraphrased ideas or concepts to a source.

- Only making minor modifications to the original wording, like deleting, rearranging, or only changing one word or part of a sentence.

As we mentioned in the introduction to this unit, our goal is not to paraphrase a source line-by-line, but rather to summarize, in our own words, the key ideas in that source. So, we wouldn't go through Burke's *Rhetoric of Motives* and extract a quote here and a quote there, nor would we try to paraphrase it line by line. Rather, we systematically go through the source and look for the key ideas. In academic research articles, we look for key aspects of the literature review, method, results, and discussion. In essays, book chapters, and websites, we look for a) the ideas that are covered by identifying the key points; b) evidence, concepts, and arguments in each main point; and c) then review the important conclusions.

2. Writing a Reference in APA Style

In addition to summarizing source content, the note-taking stage is also a good time to create a complete reference for each source in APA format. This is good practice for students who are new to APA style.

Here are some general rules for references in APA style:

- Double space everything
- Use a hanging indent for the second line, and every line thereafter

Helpful Hint

Look at the headings throughout the source to find the key ideas.

Sections of academic publications are often labeled with clear headings. The authors will also likely use second and third level headings to signal their main arguments or the key variables and their most important conclusions. Use these headings to create an outline of the source and direct your note taking.

© Odua Images, 2014. Shutterstock, Inc.

Read a main section, then take notes on what you just read. Do that for each relevant or important section of the source. This should help you be thorough while also avoiding too much reliance on direct quotes.

- Use one space after periods
- Use only first initials, middle initials, and last names for authors
- Nothing is underlined or bolded
- The titles of books and journals are italicized, and the names of books, movies, and TV shows within the title are italicized, but nothing else is italicized
- Use "n.d." if no date is given

There are numerous resources to help you with APA style on the internet and in print:

Check out Purdue University's online writing lab for help with APA style: http://owl.english.purdue.edu/

The APA also has a website with updates on APA style: http://www.apastyle.org/

The APA offers tutorials on APA style: http://www.apastyle.org/learn/tutorials/basics-tutorial.aspx

Resources to help with APA Style

Or you can purchase the APA style guide:

American Psychological Association. (2009). *Publication manual of the American Psychological Association* (6th ed.). Washington, DC: American Psychological Association.

a. Journal Articles

What you'll need for a reference for a **journal article:**

- Authors' last names, first initials, and middle initials
- Year the article was published
- Title of the article
- Title of the journal
- Volume number
- The article's first and last page numbers
- doi

Article with one author: Lastname, F. M. (YEAR). Title of the article: Follow the rules. *Journal Name, V#,* p-p. doi:ListIfGiven

Article with two authors: Lastname, F. M., & Lastname, F. M. (YEAR). Title of article: Follow the rules. *Journal Name, V#,* p-p. doi:ListIfGiven

Article with three or more authors: Lastname, F. M., Lastname, F. M., & Lastname, F. M. (YEAR). Title of the article: Follow the rules. *Journal Name, V#,* p-p. doi:ListIfGiven

APA rules:

1. Use only last names, first initial, and middle initial (if given). No first names!
2. There is a comma between every author's name.
3. There is an ampersand (&) before the last author's last name.
4. Use only the year of publication.
5. Only the first word of the title, first word of the subtitle, proper nouns, and acronyms are capitalized in the article title.
6. Every important word in the journal name is capitalized.
7. The journal name is italicized.
8. Give the volume number that the article appears in, and italicize it.
9. Give the first and last page number for the article.
10. Give the doi, if available.

Example Journal Article References:

Farley, S. D., & Stasson, M. F. (2003). Relative influences of affect and cognition on behavior: Are feelings or beliefs more related to blood donation intentions? *Experimental Psychology, 50,* 55–62. doi:10.1027//1618-3169.50.1.55

Sidelinger, R. J., Ayash, G., Gordorhazy, A., & Tibbles, D. (2008). Couples go online: Relational maintenance behaviors and relational characteristics use in dating relationships. *Human Communication, 11*, 341–356.

b. Chapters in Edited Books

What you'll need for a reference for a chapter in an **edited book**:

- Authors' last names, first initials, and middle initials
- Title of the book chapter
- Title of the book
- First and last page numbers of the chapter
- Editors' last names, first initials, and middle initials
- Year of publication
- Place of publication
- Name of publisher

Chapter with one author: Lastname, F. M. (YEAR). Title of the chapter: Follow the rules. In F. M. Editor (Ed.), *Book title* (pp. 1-2). Location: Publisher.

Chapter with two authors and two editors: Lastname, F. M., & Lastname, F. M. (YEAR). Title of the chapter: Follow the rules. In F. M. Editor & F. M. Editor (Ed.s), *Book title* (pp. 1-2). Location: Publisher.

APA Rules:

1. Use only last names, first initials, and middle initials (if given). No first names!
2. There is a comma between every author's name.
3. There is an ampersand (&) before the last author's last name.
4. Use only the year of publication.
5. Only the first word of the title, first word of the subtitle, proper nouns, and acronyms are capitalized in the chapter and book titles.
6. The book title is italicized.
7. Give the first and last page number for the chapter.
8. Give the city and state (use an abbreviation for the state) where the publication is from.
9. Give the name of the publisher.

Example Book Chapter References:

Varallo, S. M. (2004). Family photographs: A generic description. In S. K. Foss (Ed.), *Rhetorical criticism: Exploration & practice* (pp. 205–211). Long Grove, IL: Waveland.

Weaver, D., McCombs, M., & Shaw, D. L. (2004). Agenda-setting research: Issues, attributes, and influences. In L. L. Kaid (Ed.), *Handbook of political communication research* (pp. 257–282). Mahwah, NJ: Lawrence Erlbaum.

c. Books

What you'll need for a reference for **a book**:

- Authors' last names, first initials, and middle initials
- Year of publication
- Title of the book
- Place of publication
- Name of publisher

Book with one author: Lastname, F. M. (YEAR). *Book title.* Location: Publisher.

Book with multiple editions: Lastname, F. M., & Lastname, F. M. (YEAR). *Book title* (2nd ed.). Location: Publisher.

APA rules for book references:

1. Use only last names, first initials, and middle initials (if given). No first names!
2. There is a comma between every author's name.
3. There is an ampersand (&) before the last author's last name.
4. Use only the year of publication.
5. Only the first word of the title, first word of the subtitle, proper nouns, and acronyms are capitalized in book titles.
6. The book title is italicized.
7. Put the edition in parentheses after the title (5th ed.) if it is anything other than the first edition.
8. Give the city and state (use an abbreviation for the state) where the publication is from.
9. Give the name of the publisher.

Example Book References:

Foss, S. J. (2004). *Rhetorical criticism: Exploration & practice* (5th ed.). Long Grove, IL: Waveland.

Gass, R. H., & Seiter, J. S. (2011). *Persuasion: Social influence and compliance gaining* (4th ed.). Boston: Allyn & Bacon.

d. Websites

What you'll need for a reference for **a website**:

- Authors' names
- Date of publication
- Title of the webpage/document
- URL for the webpage

Website reference:

Lastname, F. M., & Lastname, F. M. (DATE). Title of webpage or document. *Name of Organization/Publication if Given.* Retrieved from http://www.websitename.com/gobbledygook

OR

Organization Name. (DATE). *Title of webpage or document.* Retrieved from http://www.websitename.com/gobbledygook

APA Rules:

1. Use only last names, first initial, and middle initial (if given). No first names!
2. When there is no author, but the website is created by an organization or company, use that information for authorship.
3. There is a comma between every author's name.
4. There is an ampersand (&) before the last author's last name.
5. Give the complete date (Year, Month, Day). Use "n.d." when there is no date.
6. Give the complete title of the document or webpage, but only the first word of the title, first word of the subtitle, proper nouns, and acronyms are capitalized.
7. Italicize the title of the webpage or document.
8. Write "Retrieved from" and give the complete URL.
9. Give as much of this information as you can, but not every website will have all of this information.

Example Website References:

Ajzen, I. (n.d.). *Theory of planned behavior.* Retrieved from http://people.umass.edu/aizen/tpb.html

McCroskey, J. C. (2007). *Communication research measures.* Retrieved from http://www.jamescmccroskey.com/measures/

Example Online Article References:

Mitchell, A., & Guskin, E. (2013). Twitter news consumers: Young, mobile, and educated. *Pew Research Journalism Project.* Retrieved from http://www.journalism.org/2013/11/04/twitter-news-consumers-young-mobile-and-educated/

C. Examples

Table 3.4   Example Completed Annotation for a Study Published in an Academic Journal

Reference in APA style:	Lee, N.-J., Shah, D. V., & McLeod, J. M. (2013). Processes of political socialization: A communication mediation approach to youth civic engagement. *Communication Research, 40*, 669–697.
Type of source:	Academic research article reporting the results of an original study
Key concepts and definitions:	• Socializing: learning about politics from parents/family, peers, classroom discussion, and the media • Communication competence: skills needed to be politically engaged • Communication mediation: social conversations and media use that affect political engagement, including news use and online content
Type of data they looked at:	Survey questions asked about: • Community service, volunteering • Political activities like voting, donating, and attending political events; how often they used traditional and online news • Frequency of online and face-to-face conversations about politics • Peer norms for politics, family conformity, and classroom discussion of politics • Demographics
Where they got their data:	Survey of American adults and their adolescent children in 2008 who were identified and contacted by a research firm that offered incentives for completing surveys.
Key findings related to each concept:	• Peer norms and classroom discussion affect following the news and discussion. Classroom discussion was most important to increasing political engagement. • Online news use increased discussion and participation, but traditional offline news use did not. This outcome was particularly pronounced for young people.
Importance and limitations of this source:	This study points to the importance of new media for promoting engaged citizens, and also added the important finding that classroom deliberation can also promote political engagement. But, some of the measures were incomplete. For example, the authors didn't look at cable news and measured news exposure but not attention.
Reference in APA style:	Delli Carpini, M. X. (2004). Mediating democratic engagement: The impact of communications on citizens' involvement in civic life. In L. L. Kaid (Ed.) *Handbook of political communication research* (pp. 395–434). Mahwah, NJ: Lawrence Erlbaum.
Type of source:	This book chapter is a literature review on engagement and involvement.

Table 3.5 Example Annotation for a Chapter in a Book/a Published Literature Review

Key concepts and definitions:	• Democratic engagement: conforming to democratic norms, being informed, participating in politics • Politically relevant media: the source, channels, and space where people collect and share political information • Political trust: trust in the government, politics, and politicians • Political alienation/cynicism: distrust of the government, politics, and politicians • Political efficacy: belief in one's ability to make a difference through voting and that voting matters • Social capital: associations with, concern and empathy for others in the community • Political interest: motivation to be politically engaged • Civic duty: sense of obligation to be politically active • Political tolerance: accepting differences, willingness to work together • Political socialization: learning political ideology from media • Political attitudes/beliefs: evaluations and beliefs about what is true • Emotions: feelings experienced in response to political information • Political/civic behavior: participating in politics
Type of data they looked at:	This is a narrative literature review.
Where they got their data:	This chapter reviews published academic research related to political engagement, attitudes, feelings, socialization, and behavior.
Key findings related to each concept:	• There is some support for the idea of "media malaise," or the notion that media can increase cynicism, though negative and cynical media seem to increase this. Research suggests that negative media content, like ads and cynical news, decreases efficacy. • Social capital increases engagement, but is declining, possibly as a result of increased media dependence. • Media socializes particular political attitudes beginning with young children. Parents also socialize children to be politically engaged. Socialization continues through adulthood, as people are influenced by friends, coworkers, and media. • Emotional reactions to information also influence attitudes and beliefs by affecting how people think about political information and what they remember. People may actually remember the emotions, but not the facts, and form opinions that way. • Different types of media affect political behavior in distinct ways: entertainment media use is related to less participation and informational media use is related to increased participation.
Importance and limitations of this source:	Engagement, trust, opinions, and behavior are related to media use and other socialization, though it is unclear whether media *causes* these outcomes. Political interest, duty, and tolerance are understudied. The demographics related to these concepts were not discussed at much length, and chances are that demographics like age, education, and income play a substantial role in trust, capital, attitudes, beliefs, and behaviors.

STEP 3

Table 3.6   Example Annotation for a Website

Reference in APA style:	Smith, A. (2013). Civic engagement in the Digital Age. Pew Internet & American Life Project. Retrieved from http://www.pewinternet.org/Reports/2013/Civic-Engagement/Summary-of-Findings.aspx.
Type of source:	Website; research by Princeton Survey Research Associates.
Key concepts and definitions:	Class: education and socioeconomic status Political activity: conversations, participating in political events, and social network activity
Type of data they looked at:	Survey questions about • Political activity (solving community problems, going to political meetings, joining a policy group, attending political rallies, volunteering for political campaigns, and participating in protests) • Demographics (age, gender, race, income, and education) • Political party affiliation and ideology • Participation online and offline in politics (signing petitions, calling in/responding to political stories, writing letters to editors)
Where they got their data:	Survey data collected from American internet users by random sampling in 2012.
Key findings related to each concept:	• Education determines political activity of all kinds • People who use social networks for political activity engage in other kinds of political activity • Political conversation is still mostly offline • Almost 40% of people participate in political activities online • Online political activity is less divided between higher and lower income/education groups • Young adults use online political activities more often, and are equally likely to participate in politics • Online politicking leads to other types of political engagement and is increasing • Political campaigns are working to contact more people online
Importance and limitations of this source:	Results show that the internet can get more people, particularly younger people, involved in politics. It's a random sample, so it's fairly representative of the American population. But, because they used a phone poll, they may not have been able to reach people who don't answer calls from unknown numbers or who hung up.

REFERENCES

American Psychological Association. (2009). *Publication manual of the American Psychological Association* (6th ed.). Washington, DC: American Psychological Association.

Shon, P. C. H. (2012). *How to read journal articles in the social sciences: A very practical guide for students.* Los Angeles: Sage.

ACTIVITIES

1. Annotations

- Write a complete annotation for an *academic journal article* using the annotation worksheet without using any quotes.
- Write a complete annotation for a *website* using the annotation worksheet without using any quotes.
- Write a complete annotation for a *book* that would be useful to your research paper using the annotation worksheet without using any quotes.

ANNOTATION WORKSHEET

Reference in APA style:	
Type of source:	
Key concepts and definitions:	
Type of data they looked at:	
Where they got their data:	
Key findings related to each concept:	
Importance and limitations of this source:	

2. Paraphrasing practice: Put the following hypotheses in your own words:

a. "The number of positive maintenance strategies used by newly married couples will be positively related to their a) satisfaction after one year of marriage and b) commitment to the relationship after one year of marriage,

STEP 3

and will be c) negatively related to their contemplation of separation and divorce after one year of marriage."

b. "There will be significant mean differences in Mean World perception between heavy television viewers and light television viewers such that a) heavy viewers will have higher estimates of the likelihood of being a victim of crime in the United States compared to light viewers; b) heavy viewers will have higher estimates of the percentage of dishonest people compared to light viewers; and c) heavy viewers will have higher estimates of the number of gun related deaths in the United States compared to light viewers."

c. "Positive affective responses (enjoyment and liking) to political ads will be higher in conditions where the advertisement mentions points of agreement with the opposition compared to ads that focus solely on points of disagreement with the opposition."

3. APA practice:

Use the following EBSCO records to write a complete reference in APA format:

a.
Title:
Bloody News and Vulnerable Populations: An Ethical Question.
Authors:
Wilkinson, Jeffrey S.
Fletcher, James E.
Source:
Journal of Mass Media Ethics; 1995, Vol. 10 Issue 3, p167, 11p
Document Type:
Article

b.
Title:
The Influence of Marital Duration on the Use of Relationship Maintenance Behaviors.
Authors:
Weigel, Daniel J.
Ballard-Reisch, Deborah S.
Source:
Communication Reports; Summer99, Vol. 12 Issue 2, p59–70, 12p, 3 Charts, 1 Graph
Document Type:
Article

STEP 4

The Fourth Step in Your Investigation: Compare, Synthesize, and Integrate the Evidence

After taking careful notes on the evidence you've collected, the next step is to begin comparing and contrasting the articles to look for patterns, just like investigators on *CSI* do when they pin up notes and pictures on a cork board in their offices during an investigation.

This step is important, because it challenges us to take a step back from looking at individual studies to considering the "bigger picture." This is when we get to do research too: qualitative research. We look at the data (sources) we have read, explore the themes and trends that emerge from their findings, and use those emergent themes to reach conclusions that integrate the evidence from your sources.

That being said, this is a difficult first step in the writing process. Sometimes it is difficult to see the forest through all the trees, or put another way, it can be difficult to figure out the specific answer to your problem question based on sometimes very different sources. In this chapter, we offer some strategies that will help you organize your sources visually and consider how all of those pieces of evidence might fit together to help you build your case.

THIS CHAPTER COVERS:

A. What is Synthesizing Evidence?
B. Why is Synthesizing Important? Because the APA says So!
C. A Componential Approach to Synthesizing Related Articles
   1. Why Use a Componential Method
   2. How to Conduct a Componential (Key Components) Analysis
   3. A Componential Synthesizing Example
D. A Directed Approach to Synthesizing When Your Paper is Guided by a Theory
   1. Why We Use a Directed Approach
   2. How to Conduct a Directed Analysis
   3. An Example Directed Analysis

In research, we look for similarities and differences in the articles we've read that help us answer our problem question and organize the evidence we've collected through our reading and note taking. Putting together articles is like putting together pieces of a puzzle, or pieces of evidence to build a case: you have to see which articles link together in a logical way, and how those pieces fit together to create one complete view of your topic. Once you see the complete picture, you can critique what you see: What is missing from the picture? What is inconsistent or unclear?

Foss and Walters (2007) suggest the following steps in combing through a pile of books and articles to organize your notes and plan your literature review: find relevant excerpts; sort excerpts into logical categories; organize your categories; create an organizational framework based on the categories; then write. We will go over this process in detail in this unit. But first, let's discuss why this is an important step.

A. What is Synthesizing Evidence?

Generally, it is not acceptable to write a paper that simply strings together annotations or summaries of sources. A well-written paper *synthesizes* the research being discussed. **Synthesizing** means bringing everything together by combining, contrasting, and integrating. This is done by comparing and contrasting article content in terms of the variables studied: We look for similarities and differences in definitions of variables, how variables are measured, or what is found. For example, the following excerpt from my own research synthesizes definitions of media use motives from uses and gratifications theory:

> After reviewing the different types of motives for news use (Greenburg, 1974; Rubin, 1984; Perse, 1992; Blumler & McQuail, 1969) one thing is clear: motives are either active reasons for using the news or passive, diversionary reasons. Greenburg's (1974) motives clearly vary in activeness. For example, the difference between using the news to "pastime" and "learn information" is clearly one of inactivity and passivity versus active use. Rubin (1984) later validated the idea that there are two "news use orientations" in motives, and Perse (1992) used Rubin's motives index to explain news use. Perse clarified that active and passive motives explain differences in media effects.

B. Why is Synthesizing Important? Because the APA Says So!

APA style guidelines suggest that we "describe relevant scholarship" and warns against having an exhaustive literature review full of unnecessary details (p. 28). Rather, literature reviews should (p. 10):

- explain the problem being researched
- *summarize* existing research
- point out how previous studies are similar, different, and what's missing in the current research
- provide a direction that research should go to solve the problem

The literature review can be organized into main points that focus on similar concepts, theories, methods, or even historical changes. But these main points should not be a recitation of all of the details in every study. Rather, we look for broad trends, or themes, in the research we have read, and our paper is a *synthesis* of those studies that lead to a series of specific conclusions about current knowledge. When we have a theory guiding our review of literature, we can use a more directed approach to synthesizing by looking at concepts and methods described in the literature we have gathered.

This process can seem daunting, as sometimes all of our sources can sound the same, such as when they all look at one specific theory using a similar method. Other times, our sources seem to be going in completely different directions, and include numerous theories, concepts, and diverse methods. Regardless of how similar or different our sources initially seem to be, we can use close, careful analysis of our written annotations to find the subtle similarities, differences, and areas of ambiguity in the research we've read.

In this book, we teach students content analytic methods that help them organize their notes (or annotations, as the case is in our classes!) to help students see the themes and trends in the sources they are using. Content analytic methods, such as the general componential approach guided by the parts of a typical academic publication and directed analysis based on the theory you are researching, help us organize, identify trends or themes, and even see what's missing in the research we are discussing. It is a way for us to further condense the information we are incorporating into our papers.

C. A Componential Approach to Synthesizing Related Articles

1. Why Use a Componential Method

A **componential approach** is a qualitative research method used to identify trends in content. We recommend a componential approach because it is a "data reduction technique," which means that you use it to take a lot of content and boil it down to find a few recurring themes within that content (Spradley, 1980). Componential methods are used when we have specific categories of information and we want to find themes, or trends, within those categories.

In your annotations, you have specific categories of information from your sources: variables/concepts, methods, and results/conclusions. Therefore, the componential approach can help you find trends in each of those areas, and the main topics or main points for your paper can emerge from all or any combination of those areas.

2. How to Conduct a Componential (Key Components) Analysis

The easiest way to find these points of comparison in your articles, and to find sub-topics for your paper, is to create a chart of the variables explored in

STEP 4

each article. To find themes in the categories, we follow these steps: Fill in the information for each of the articles you've selected to include in your literature review. Rather than cutting and pasting from the annotations, put the information in a *brief form*, as shown in the example below. When you have your articles listed, highlight *similar* terms, concepts, findings, and methods. Consider trying a color-coding scheme, where similar concepts are highlighted in a particular color.

So, there are four steps to conducting a componential analysis of your annotated references:

1. Create a chart with four columns: Article, Variables/Concepts, Method, Findings
2. Read through your annotations several times: Once for variables/concepts, again for methods, and again for findings. Make notes in each column for each article as you are reading through your annotations.
3. Look at each category in your chart: What trends do you see in variables/concepts? What trends do you see in methods? What trends do you see in results?
4. Highlight trends using a color-coding scheme with one unique color for each *type* of variable/concept, each type of method, and each key finding.

Using a chart helps you see similar variables that are covered in different articles. Using the chart, and during the process of continually reading and rereading the notes on your articles, you will typically find trends in the research. Articles may be similar in variables, method, and/or findings. These similarities, or trends, will become your main points for the final paper. Some of the studies you reviewed may *define* variables similarly or differently, introduce *different* types of variables, *measure* the same variables differently, or *find* different relationships between variables. These similarities and differences will be used to develop your synthesis and comparison and contrast in the final literature review.

3. A Componential Synthesizing Example

In this example, the Theory of Planned Behavior, gratifications/motives, and affect are the concepts we see coming up repeatedly. We also see that the methodology is similar among these articles: all but one are survey studies. So, by looking at the chart, we see that there are several themes in the literature: motives, emotions, and theory of planned behavior variables predict political news use and political behaviors. Also, we see an important potential critique of this literature: these are all survey studies, which have inherent limitations.

Table 4.1 Componential Synthesizing Example

Article	Concepts	Data	Findings/Conclusions
1. Rubin (1984)	Motives and media use	Survey	Found active and passive grats
2. Palmgreen & Rayburn (1984)	Gratifications sought/obtained Affect/beliefs	Survey of adult news users	Grats and beliefs determine news genre selection according to TPB
3. Lavine et al. (1998)	Cognitive attitudes Affective attitudes Voting decisions	Survey of adult voters that used scale measures	Cognition and affect will determine vote choice. Affect superseded cognition.
4. Herr (1999)	Affect and the theory of planned behavior	Review/critique of literature	Affect may be the outcome of belief, or may determine beliefs in TPB
5. Rivis et al. (2009)	Affect and TPB variables	Meta-analysis of previous survey studies	Affect not related to TPB variables; is related to behavior

D. A Directed Approach to Synthesizing When Your Paper is Guided by a Theory

1. Why We Use a Directed Approach

We use componential analyses when we aren't sure what the main concepts are going to be that we focus on in our final paper. But when there is a theory guiding our research, then the theory prescribes the main concepts we should focus on. Therefore, when your paper is guided by a theory, then a directed approach to synthesizing articles is in order. Typically, a theory has specific concepts and explains how those concepts fit together. Therefore, rather than using an open coding method like componential analysis, we can instead conduct a **directed analysis** where we focus on the specific concepts outlined in the theory we are researching. Directed analysis is a way to organize content into clearly predefined categories that are based on existing theory (Hseih & Shannon, 2005).

2. How to Conduct a Directed Analysis

In directed analysis, you begin by looking at how each article contributes to our understanding of one or more concepts from the theory. So, we list the concepts from the theory, then we make a note of which articles looked at those specific concepts and how they looked at them.

Therefore, the steps in a directed analysis are:

1. List the key concepts for your theory in the top row.
2. Working in chronological order, note which articles looked at each of those key concepts, how they looked at them, and what they found.

3. Look for trends and subthemes in the research on each theory-related concept.
4. Highlight different subthemes in the research in each category.
5. Look for concepts that are under-researched compared to other concepts.

Much like the general componential approach to exploring how our sources fit together, a chart is useful for a directed analysis as well. We can have one column in the chart for each concept in our theory, and the rows can each be one of the articles we're looking at for our paper.

3. An Example Directed Analysis

In this example of articles focusing on the theory of planned behavior, we see trends emerging: there are specific variables related to the general concepts in the theory (cognitive and affective are *types* of attitudes); also, there are areas (like subjective norms and perceived behavioral control) that are under-developed compared to other concepts.

Table 4.2   Directed Analysis Example

Source	Concept 1: Attitudes	Concept 2: Norms	Concept 3: Behavioral Control	Extensions/ Implications
Lavine et al. (1998) Survey	Cognitive and affective attitudes predict voting			Affect predicts behavior
Herr (1999) Review	Affect may be an outcome of attitudes or may predict them			Unclear whether affect happens before or after attitudes
Delli Carpini (2004). Review	Emotions and information are related to attitudes and each other		Political efficacy determines engagement.	Efficacy, emotions, and socialization are key to increasing political engagement
Rivis et al. (2009) Meta-analysis	Affect predicts attitudes	Affect not related to norms	Affect not related to behavioral control	Affect predicts attitudes, not other TPB variables
Lee et al. (2013) Survey		Norms affect engagement	Communication competence is learning the skills needed to be engaged	Socialization happens in classrooms and among peers. New media increases engagement.

Notice in this example that we categorize content from the articles based on *similar concepts*, because not all of the articles have the *exact same* concepts. For example, under behavioral control, we include both efficacy and competence / skills, as these are related to a person's sense of behavioral control. We know these fit here because we have carefully noted the definitions of behavioral control, efficacy, and competence when reading our articles and so we recognize that these definitions overlap. When discussing behavioral control in the literature review, we would talk about both having a sense of political efficacy and developing competence as they relate to whether young people feel a sense of behavioral control or not.

REFERENCES

Foss, S. K., & Waters, W. (2007). *Destination dissertation: A traveler's guide to a done dissertation.* Lanham, MD: Rowman & Littlefield.

Hsieh, H.-F., & Shannon, S.E. (2005). Three approaches to qualitative content analysis. *Qualitative Health Research, 15(9)*, 1277–1288.

Spradley, J. P. (1979). *The ethnographic interview.* New York: Holt, Rinehart & Winston.

ACTIVITIES

1. An Annotation Word Cloud

Copy and paste your completed annotations into a word cloud program, such as www.wordle.net. What words are coming up repeatedly? These may be the main themes in your sources.

For example, a word cloud of our example annotations looks like this:

Wordle

Notice in this word cloud from Wordle.net that media, engagement, discussion, online, activity, news, and education are our largest words other than "political." These are the most frequently occurring terms in our annotations. The next level includes demographics, attitudes, education, trust, socialization, information, and participation.

So, thinking about this a different way, the most prominent words seem to the independent variables such as demographics, education, and socialization, and dependent variables such as engagement, activity, and participation.

2. Qualitative Content Analysis of Your Notes

Complete a synthesizing worksheet, such as the Key Components Worksheet or Theory-Directed Worksheet provided here. Choose a color-coding scheme, where similar terms are highlighted in the same color. What colors are you seeing the most? What colors are you seeing the least? Answering these questions will help you identify the themes, and the areas of needed research, for your main points and criticisms of the literature.

Key Components Worksheet

Article	Concepts	Data	Findings/ Conclusions
1.			
2.			
3.			
4.			
5.			
6.			
7.			

8.			
9.			
10.			

Theory-Directed Worksheet

Source Info:	Concept 1:	Concept 2:	Concept 3:	Concept 4:	Implications
1.					
2.					
3.					
4.					
5.					
6.					

7.					
8.					
9.					
10.					

STEP 5

The Fifth Step in Your Investigation: Outline the Case You've Built

Kallan (2013) argued that we should write for an audience that is "tired and cranky, bored by your subject, opposed to your position, and hostile toward you" (p. 5). This may seem like odd advice, but he is correct that all writing, including writing literature reviews, is fundamentally persuasive. If we think of our reader as disinterested or even hostile, we are likely going to make a more compelling case for our conclusions: We will be motivated to make the clearest, most convincing case we possibly can. We make a clear and compelling case by beginning with a strong introduction; having clear, interrelated, and well-supported main points; and offering a solid, meaningful conclusion based on the arguments in each main point.

THIS CHAPTER COVERS:

A. Writing a Compelling Introduction
B. Developing your Argument
   1. The Toulmin Model
C. Citing Sources: A Basic Overview
   1. Types of In-Text Citations
   2. APA Rules for In-Text Citations
D. Organizing Main Points
   1. The Topical Review: Explaining and Critiquing the Concepts, Findings, or Methods
   2. The Comparison / Contrast Review: Comparing Different Explanations
   3. The Chronology of Research: Historical Reviews
   4. The Sequential Process: Explaining a Sequence of Events or Outcomes
   5. The Cause-Effect Approach: Explaining a Direct, Causal Process
   6. The Direct Argument: Arguing for a New Theory or Specific Policy
E. Using Transitions
F. Setting up Hypotheses and/or Research Questions
G. Writing a Good Conclusion
   1. Recapping Your Argument
   2. Writing a Meaningful, Insightful Conclusion

A. Writing a Compelling Introduction

The introduction and conclusion both serve a purpose similar to the transition statement: they remind your reader where you're going in the paper and what your point is. In the introduction, get your audience's interest by having some attention-getting statement, like a startling statistic, quote, or idea that they may find intriguing. Next, clearly state the purpose of your paper in the thesis statement. A good introduction also clearly lets the reader know the importance of examining this topic. For example, this might be a largely ignored area in the research, or you may have a new approach to an old problem. Finally, in the introduction, preview each of your main points in the order they will appear in your paper.

TIP

Remember, if you can't gain someone's interest in the introduction, they are unlikely to read the rest of the paper. Presenting your best argument right up front and delivering on that argument throughout your paper will ensure your work is clearly understood.

© cosmo, 2014. Shutterstock, Inc.

An introduction includes a:

- Statement that gets your reader's attention
- Thesis, or overarching goal, of your paper
- Statement about the importance of your topic
- Preview of the main points in your paper

B. Developing Your Argument

When writing a literature review, you may see it as a mere reporting of facts; you are simply finding existing research and putting it together for your reader. However, this is not really the case. A literature review should be focused and have a clear purpose. As mentioned in the beginning of this chapter, essentially when you write a literature review, you are building a persuasive argument. You are not simply summarizing each study you run across that might support your points. The goal is to synthesize (see Step 4 of this book)—to have main points that will clearly outline your argument and use existing research as support for those main points.

1. The Toulmin Model

In order to help you build your argument, it is useful to examine the Toulmin Model of argumentation. This model was developed by Stephen Toulmin in 1958, and is still used today to formulate cohesive, strong, logical arguments (Hitchcock & Verheij, 2005). The Toulmin Model essentially assesses a claim and breaks it down to ensure that the claim is valid through the use of credible evidence. Additionally, the Toulmin Model incorporates the use of rebuttal as a method of strengthening an argument. In the case of a literature review, a rebuttal might be acknowledging weaknesses in the literature or theories, but then counter-arguing how these weaknesses can be overcome.

The Toulmin Model is useful not only in determining your main points and outlining your entire paper, but once you have determined those points, you can apply the model to arguing within each main point. Figure 5.1 outlines the main components of the Toulmin Model.

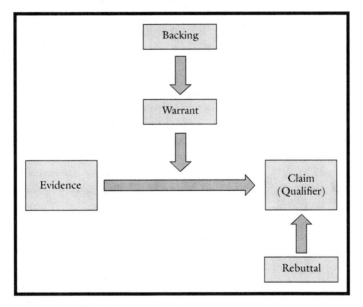

Figure 5.1   The Toulmin Model.

Let's break down each component of the model as it relates to writing a literature review. First, the **claim**. The claim is your assertion, or the point that you wish to make (Toulmin, 2003). It is the answer to the question you posed at the start of your writing project. You can apply this model to your overall paper (in which case, your claim would be your thesis statement) as well as each main point. In order for an argument to have sound logic, the claim has to be

STEP 5

true. We can make claims more "true" if we use qualifiers, or words that make a statement more flexible and/or tentative. For example, I could make the claim "Watching violent television always leads children to be aggressive." As you can imagine, it would be easy to refute this claim, because not all children who watch violent TV become aggressive. However, if I use a qualifier, this statement actually becomes stronger. I could say "Children who watch violent television *might* become more aggressive." This statement is harder to refute, because it is true that some kids do become more violent after exposure to violent media. Other qualifiers include some, few, might, may, likely/unlikely, probably, etc. Because communication research focuses on human behavior and interactions, it is difficult to make definitive statements that include words like always or never. Therefore, qualifiers are particularly useful when making arguments regarding communication studies.

The next component of the model is **evidence**. Evidence is the foundation or grounding for making your claim; it is the facts that support your main assertion (Karbach, 1987). When deciding on which main points to include as evidence for your overall argument (your thesis), look back to the work you completed in Step 4. The main points of your paper should come from the trends in articles that you found in the synthesizing project. Groups of articles may be similar in that they all look at one specific variable, look at a common type of variable, use a similar methodology, or have similar results. These small trends will be your main points, or main arguments, in your paper.

Try several ways of grouping your articles together to see how they fit together best: Which groupings of the articles most clearly highlight the trends you found in the research? Which trends are most important to you and your research purpose? Your answer to these two questions should determine the main points in your paper. Kallan (2013) likens this process to creating "piles" and "subpiles" of your evidence (p. 49).

It is important to remember that each main point also has a thesis, or subthesis, and therefore will also require an argument. Within your main point, you will need to provide evidence to support that claim. Remember that you are not writing an annotated bibliography, or simply summarizing each article you wish to use as support. It is important that our papers *not* read like a series of strung-together annotations. You should look at the evidence you have gathered, and like you did for determining your overall main points, look for common threads amongst articles. The strongest form of evidence when arguing for a main point is going to be study results. Be sure to focus on this aspect of the research you gathered.

Remember

Part of being clear in making your argument is to define any important terms or variables that you are discussing. Research studies may include jargon that not all readers will understand. When in doubt, define and explain. Avoid assuming everyone is a communication scholar; your work should be accessible to a large audience.

© Archiwiz, 2014. Shutterstock, Inc.

When writing a literature review, the **warrant** is a vital step. The warrant is the "explanation of why or how the data supports the claim" (Weida & Stolley, 2013). Often referred to as "the bridge," the warrant connects the support (main points, evidence) to your claim (thesis). Typically, when writing a literature review, the warrant is explicitly stated. Take a look at the example outline provided at the end of this chapter. Notice how a conclusion statement is given for each main point, as well as for the entire paper. These claims help serve as the warrant for the arguments provided. **Backing** is then the support for the warrant. As you can see, the key to a strong argument is support. A warrant, just like a claim, may need additional evidence to support it.

Lastly, you should include the **rebuttal,** or the response to any counter-arguments to your position. All research has limitations, weaknesses, and criticisms. Your job as a good writer is to know these criticisms and to discuss how your thesis will be strong despite any flaws. In a literature review situation, this might include your rationale for choosing one theoretical perspective over another, or including a thorough comparison and contrast of the articles you are choosing as support within a main point. The rebuttal is also evident in the discussion section, when you detail your own limitations and/or conclusions. Good research is honest and transparent; flaws should be acknowledged and explained so that accurate conclusions can be drawn.

Based upon Toulmin's Model, your main points should:

- All be related to the one overarching claim, or thesis, for your paper
- Include thorough, credible support
- Be a synthesis of studies, *not* a recitation of your abstracts
- Include definitions of key variables, concepts, and theories as they are discussed
- Address any counter-arguments that may arise

C. Citing Sources: A Basic Overview

In order to support your claims and warrants, you must cite credible sources. One of the most useful aspects of having an outline written is that it also organizes the source evidence that you've found. This section will give you some basic structure for how to cite sources as you put together your outline and, ultimately, use that outline to write your paper. Citation enhances your credibility, and therefore strengthens your argument. Of course, the best place to learn about citation is the proper style guide. As we discussed earlier, the communication discipline follows the American Psychological Association (APA) style guide; therefore, the examples below are in APA style. For further instruction, see the latest edition of the APA manual, or visit http://www.apastyle.org/.

APA manual

1. Types of In-Text Citations

Throughout our writing, we should always give credit where credit is due, and that includes citing sources as we use their ideas, concepts, or theories in our papers. One way that we "give credit" in writing is by clearly citing sources as we use sources in our paper. In-text citations will typically be parenthetical, but may also be written as part of a sentence. Parenthetical literally means "using parentheses," and these in-text citations are usually put at the end of the sentence. On the other hand, we can include the authors' names in the sentence, then only the year is in parentheses.

Parenthetical in-text citation examples:
- Parenthetical with one author: Research has suggested that students despise APA (Curnalia, 2009).
- Parenthetical with two authors: Subsequent studies clarified that learning these rules helps students grow as writers (Curnalia & Ferris, 2009).
- Parenthetical with three or more authors: Ultimately, whether one is writing a blog, writing press releases, or emailing clients, being able to write effectively and correctly is an essential life skill (Curnalia, Ferris, & Angryundergrad, 2009).

Citations within sentences:
- In a sentence with one author: Curnalia (2009) found that students despise APA.
- In a sentence with two authors: Curnalia and Ferris (2009) found that learning these rules helps students grow as writers.
- In a sentence with three or more authors: Curnalia, Ferris, and Angryundergrad (2009) argued that, whether one is writing a blog, press releases, or emailing clients, being able to write effectively and correctly is an essential life skill.

The *et al.* **rule**. When there are three, four, or five authors, cite them all the first time you use that source. After that, you use the first author's last name followed by et al. If there are six or more authors, use the first author's last name followed by et al. every time you cite that source.

- First time you mention the article: Curnalia, Ferris, Smith, Jones, and Angryundergrad (2014) found that students despise APA.
- Second time you mention the article: Curnalia et al. (2014) found that learning these rules helps students grow as writers.

Citations for a quote. Generally, direct quotes are avoided when writing a literature review; your main focus should be on paraphrasing. When you must use a quote, use quotation marks around the quoted text and give the page number that the quote is from in the parenthetical citation. For example, "*Students reported genuinely loathing APA for its persnickety rules" (Curnalia, 2009, p. 4)*. Note that the period for the sentence always goes after the in-text citation.

2. APA Rules for In-text Citations

When to cite. We give a citation for any idea, opinion, concept, theory, definition, or explanation that is taken from or based upon another person's work. Whether it is a website, email exchange, or academic writing, we need to make it clear to our reader where content originated. We do this for a couple of reasons. First, it is the ethical thing to do. We have an ethical obligation to give people credit for their ideas and their work. Second, citing relevant, credible sources bolsters your own credibility. When you provide support for your arguments, you are letting the reader know that they do not just have to trust your word, but others support you as well. Lastly, in academics, generating citations is an important way for us to track the impact of our scholarship.

We often think that plagiarism is merely using unmarked quotes. The APA explains, "do not present portions of another's work or data as [your] own, even if the other work or data source is cited occasionally" (APA, 8.11). Further, in the APA style guide, it states:

> "*plagiarism* refers to the practice of claiming credit for the words, ideas, and concepts of others" (Publication Manual, 2009, 6.02). When you are "paraphrasing, quoting an author directly, or describing an idea...you must credit the source" (Publication Manual, 2009, 6.01).

Where to cite. We do not need to cite in every sentence. As a general rule of thumb, it must be clear where our information is from. Therefore, we cite authors:

- In the sentence where we first refer to their work
- At the beginning of new paragraphs where we are continuing a discussion of a particular article
- When we are moving between one source and another source.

For example, we might write the following:

> Curnalia and Ferris (2014) point out that in-text citations are essential as you start to build your literature review, beginning with your writing outline. The APA *Publication Manual* (2009) explains that this is an ethical issue. Curnalia and Ferris (2014) go on to explain that in-text citations are also essential in terms of building a convincing argument. So, in sum, in-text citations are essential to effective and ethical writing.

Authors' first names and initials. As a general rule only use authors' last names. The one exception to this rule is when you have different authors with the same last name. In that case, you can use the first initial of the authors who have the same last name. For example, if I had an article by A. Anderson and an article by M. Anderson, I would use their first initials in the paper so that it is clear which of the two authors I am referring to at different points in my paper. Generally, we do not use first names in the paper, and first names should not appear in your in-text citations or your reference list.

D. Organizing Main Points

Once you have your main points, you need to decide how to address them most effectively in your paper. There are several options, depending on the types of trends you found. If you found that studies were changing as time progressed (research was moving in a particular direction over time), then use a chronological pattern where you take us through that process of change. If you found that there are groupings of variables that are similar, and all are equally important, then use a topical organizational pattern where each main point is discussed in relatively equal depth. If there is one main point that seems particularly important, you can start with that as your first point then arrange other points in order of their importance. Finally, you could build up to your most important point using smaller, less consequential points. Choose the organizational pattern that best fits your topic and your purpose.

You have several options for how you approach your paper based on the themes you found during your analysis of the academic literature (Miller, 2007): Create topics, compare and contrast, explain a chronology or process, explain causes and effects, or argue for a new theory. We will discuss all of these in some detail below.

1. The Topical Review: Explaining and Critiquing the Concepts, Findings, or Methods

The most common type of literature review summarizes research on a few interrelated main topics. These literature reviews are not always *exhaustive* (they don't include every study ever done on every topic in the paper), but they do involve *thoroughly* covering each related topic.

If your literature review is more conceptual, meaning that it is focused on defining related concepts or dimensions of a single concept, then a topical review may be your best option for main points. Similarly, if you are summarizing the key findings in a particular area of research, then each main point in your paper can focus on a subset of similar findings or conclusions in the literature. Lastly, if you are writing a methodological critique, one option is to discuss the different methods used in related studies in separate main points.

2. The Comparison / Contrast Review: Comparing Different Explanations

Many times, there are competing explanations of some communication outcome. Two or more theories or areas of research may explain the same process or communication effects differently. For example, some researchers explain relationship satisfaction as an outcome of relationship maintenance; other researchers explain satisfaction as the result of rewards, costs, meeting expectations, and comparison to alternatives. In media research, some theorists argue that motives determine effects, other researchers argue that media content causes effects. These types of topics, where there are competing or complementary explanations of the communication outcome being researched, offer the opportunity to compare and contrast in our literature review.

3. The Chronology of Research: Historical Reviews

A chronological approach may be appropriate if you wish to show how a topic has changed or evolved over time. Chronologies can start from the most recent literature on a subject and move backward in time, or they might start with the original works and move toward where the topic currently stands. This approach can be used with any subject, from examining the evolution of a particular medium to the development of a specific variable or theory. For example, you might write a literature review on the history of radio research from the technology's inception to now. Or, you might discuss the past, present, and future of research on the theory of reasoned action.

The key in this pattern is time order; how you choose to break up segments of time will vary depending on your topic. If you are talking about social networking research, one to five year increments might be appropriate. Other topics that have been extensively researched for long periods of time, such as Aristotle's concepts of ethos, logos, and pathos, may require longer intervals.

4. The Sequential Process: Explaining a Sequence of Events or Outcomes

Similar to a chronological approach, a sequential process pattern is also based on time. The difference is that rather than focusing on increments of time, your main points are organized in steps or key events. When you are describing a process, this pattern is most appropriate. For example, you might be writing a literature review on the stages of relationships. One way to organize this review would be to start with the initiation of the relationship, maintaining the relationship, and then dissolution of the relationship. As you can see from this example, the stages of relationships follow a specific order where the preceding step must be achieved before the next step will make sense. Any topic that includes models or stages would be an appropriate fit for a sequential outcome.

Another application of the sequential pattern could be to discuss the key events in a particular variable, theory, or perspective's evolution. For example, you could trace the development of the theory of reasoned action or the spiral of silence. Or, you could outline how the definition of violence has changed over time. The important difference between the sequential and the chronological approach is how you phrase your main points. You could outline the definition of violence based on decade (chronological) or you could discuss the key points where the definition changed (Gerbner's original definition, addition of animated violence, verbal aggression, etc.). Both are time-ordered, but the latter focuses on events rather than eras.

5. The Cause-Effect Approach: Explaining a Direct, Causal Process

The cause-effect pattern is often used when you wish to show several causes that might lead to a potential effect, or several effects that result from a common cause. It is rare in communication research that any one effect is linked to one cause and vice versa. In reality, experimental or longitudinal research studies are the only designs capable of showing cause and effect. Additionally, you want to be sure to exhibit caution when making claims of causality, particularly when the direction of a cause could be debatable. For example, many people argue that violent video games cause people to be aggressive; however, it is just as plausible that aggressive people play violent video games.

Often times, it is more useful to show links or relationships between variables when writing a literature review. For example, you might review literature on what leads to increased worker satisfaction in organizations or what effects junk food advertisements have on children. In this case, your main points will focus on building a case for the cause and effect link. For example, if you wanted to claim that positive teaching evaluations are related to professor behavior (i.e., professor behavior causes positive evaluations), your main points might focus on instructor verbal and nonverbal immediacy behaviors in relation to student perceptions.

6. The Direct Argument: Arguing for a New Theory or Specific Policy

The direct argument is a type of persuasive organizational pattern used to argue for a specific idea or point. This option is most commonly used for arguing that scholars should adopt a new theory, policy, or way of thinking. Essentially, you should apply the Toulmin Model discussed at the beginning of this chapter in order to convince your readers of your proposal. You will have a claim, and your main points should each support that claim. For example, you might choose to argue for a change in how doctors engage with their patients based on communication research. Your main points should focus on what types of evidence would be necessary to convince doctors to change, and should be supported with research results that "prove" you are right. You should clearly define the warrant, as well as show any opposition to your argument and give a rebuttal for any opposing views.

Overall, the important factor to keep in mind when choosing an organizational pattern is that there is no "right" way to write a literature review. The pattern you choose should depend on the purpose for writing the review and the goal you hope to achieve in the end. Once you have a pattern and have outlined your main points, the next key component of a literature review is to incorporate effective transitions.

E. Using Transitions

Your reader should always know where you're going in your paper and how these ideas are related to each other. It is your job as a writer to explain this to your reader explicitly throughout the paper. **Transition statements** are sentences that signal to your reader that you're moving on, by briefly summarizing what was just discussed and previewing what will be discussed next. We put transition statements between the introduction and the body of the paper, each of the main points (and often between sub-points within main points when we're moving between articles), and between the body and the conclusion. Good transitions allow the reader to follow your argument easily; the harder your paper is to follow, the greater the chance your point will be lost. You don't want the reader to be left wondering why we moved on from one topic to another and where we're going next.

F. Setting Up Hypotheses and/or Research Questions

In some instances, you may be asked to derive hypotheses and/or research questions based on the literature you have reviewed. When conducting a full study (including a method and results section), research questions and hypotheses typically follow the literature review (although there certainly are variations to this approach). There are two things that this section might accomplish: 1) Explain to your audience what specific conclusions can be reached based on the studies you have reviewed. 2) Point out any ambiguities, or what things are unclear or untested, that need to be cleared up in the literature.

Conclusions, which we reach based on articles with similar variables, methods, and results, become our hypotheses because we can state with some certainty that specific relationships will be found. For example, you may have found that research consistently reports that women communicate for relational purposes and men for instrumental purposes. If you can safely make this prediction within the context of mobile phone use, then you could propose a hypothesis about gender differences in mobile phone use.

When there is an ambiguity (like variables being measured differently, or different results being found, or variables not being explored that may be important) we pose a research question because we cannot, with confidence, project how those variables may be related. For example, some studies might show that some demographic variables impact parent-child communication strategies, whereas others do not. Or, demographics might not have been examined in this body of research. In either case, because you cannot with certainty make a prediction, a research question is more appropriate.

When proposing hypotheses or research questions, it is important to provide a rationale prior to or after the question/statement is made. That rationale should include a synthesis of the research you have previously gathered and incorporated in the literature review. You should clearly incorporate your main points into the reasoning behind your proposed hypotheses. If a main point is not evident in at least one of your hypotheses or research questions, this is a clear sign that you did not need that point in your review. After you have made your predictions, your next step is to conclude your paper.

G. Writing a Good Conclusion

Like your introduction, your conclusion is a key section of your literature review. There are two main goals of a conclusion: to recap your main points and to draw meaningful conclusions based on these main points.

1. Recapping Your Main Argument

In the conclusion, you essentially restate and summarize your argument. The first thing you should do is recap your main points and restate your thesis. It is important to note that you are not simply copying and pasting what you wrote in the beginning to the end of your paper. You are reminding the reader of the key "takeaway" points from your work in order to reiterate your argument.

It is also useful in the conclusion to recap some of the important components discussed in your main points, including any important findings or conclusions that you have drawn from this literature in regards to your thesis. You should restate why it is important to study this topic, and include support from your paper.

Lastly, you want to leave the reader with a lasting impression of your work. This is achieved by writing a meaningful concluding paragraph. The following section will provide further detail on how to accomplish this task.

2. Writing a Meaningful, Insightful Conclusion

In addition to making an argument, a literature review should really provoke thought and further exploration from the reader. You have reiterated your main points, made the case again for why your topic is important—now your job is to inspire the reader. This is your chance to propose future directions for research on this topic and to add insight to this area of study. Think of any areas where the research could be expanded or areas that have not been explored that deserve our attention. Consider the implications for your review to the practical world—what does it mean to know that gender differences affect self-disclosure? Or that video games have been shown to increase learning capacity in children? Or that speaking anxiety is lessened by deep breathing techniques?

You don't want to be overly dramatic or overstate the reach of your findings, but you do want to put your argument into perspective. It is acceptable to recap the counter-argument to your findings in order to have a final rebuttal. In fact, acknowledging weaknesses in the literature or in the argument can provide great opportunities for suggestions to extend the research in a particular area. What you do not want to do in a conclusion is simply recap your points and end it there. If you can leave the reader excited about your topic and thinking of ways to expand upon it, your conclusion (and ultimately your literature review) was a success.

REFERENCES

American Psychological Association. (2009). Ethical principles of psychologists and code of conduct. Retrieved from http://www.apa.org/ethics/code/index.aspx.

Hitchcock, D., & Verheij, B. (2005). The Toulmin Model today: Introduction to the special issue on contemporary work using Stephen Edelston Toulmin's layout of arguments. *Argumentation, 19,* 255–258. doi: 10.1007/s10503-005-4414y

Kallan, R. (2013). *Renovating your writing: Shaping ideas into clear, concise, and compelling messages.* Upper Saddle River, NJ: Pearson.

Karbach, J. (1987). Using Toulmin's Model of argumentation. *Journal of Teaching Writing, 6,* 81–91.

Miller, G. (2007). *The Prentice Hall reader* (8th ed.). Upper Saddle River, NJ: Pearson.

Publication manual of the American Psychological Association (6th ed.). (2009). Washington, DC: American Psychological Association.

Toulmin, S. E. (2003). *The Uses of Argument* (updated ed.). Cambridge, UK: Cambridge University Press.

Weida, S., & Stolley, K. (2013, March). Organizing your argument. *Purdue University Online Writing Lab.* Retrieved from https://owl.english.purdue.edu/owl/resource/588/03/

Example Literature Review Outline

Introduction:

- *Attention-getting statement*: Many researchers and politicians are concerned that younger people do not follow politics and are not politically active.
- *Thesis / purpose*: This paper addresses the research on political activity to explore some of the reasons people are more or less likely to be engaged in American politics.
- *Statement of importance*: By better understanding how and why people follow politics, researchers will be able to make recommendations about how to get more young people interested and, hopefully, get more young people voting in elections.
- *Preview of main points*: Two theories are discussed that help explain how and why people follow the news and participate in politics: motives for news use and the theory of planned behavior (TPB).

First Main Point: Motives for Political News Use

- Section thesis: There are different types of motives for media use identified in news research.
- Evidence:
  - For example, Greenberg (1974) used open-ended questions to create a typology of television viewing motives for British children. Eight viewing motives were identified: passing time, diversion, to learn about the world, to learn about oneself, for arousal, relaxation, companionship, and habit.
  - Rubin (1984) and Perse (1992) identified ritualistic and instrumental motives from a typology that was similar to Greenberg's (1974).
  - Palmgreen and Rayburn (1984) looked at keeping up with issues, finding out about officials, entertainment, support viewpoints to others, news casters' human quality, share information with others, drama, compare own ideas, conversational topics, excitement, reports being like others I know, making up my mind, trustworthy information, and finding out about issues that may affect me.
- Section conclusion: After reviewing the different types of motives for news use introduced by Greenberg (1974) and Rubin (1984) and Perse (1992), and Palmgreen and Rayburn (1984), one thing is clear: motives are either active reasons for using the news or passive, diversionary reasons. They include a combination of cognitive and affective reasons for using news media.

[Transition: Motives affect what we watch, and the TPB predicts what we do.]

Second Main Point: The Theory of Planned Behavior

- Section thesis: Ajzen (1985) introduced the theory of planned behavior (TPB) to explain how individuals' attitudes are related to their behavior.
  - According to the TPB, people's intentions to perform a behavior such as watching the news are the result of three individual judgments: a) Attitude toward the behavior, including beliefs about the expected outcomes of the behavior and the strength of beliefs; b) norms for the behavior and motivation to comply with that normative pressure; and c) the perception that one is able to perform the behavior, or has behavioral control.
- Evidence:
  - Beliefs vary in favorability (Durnan & Trafimow, 2000) and have both affective (evaluative) and cognitive (informational) aspects (Lavine, Thomsen, Zanna, & Borgida, 1998).
  - Rivis et al. (2009) and Herr (1999) said that affect is an important part of predicting behavior in addition to beliefs, norms, and perceived behavioral control. Lavine et al. (1998) also found that affect may be more important than cognitive beliefs in some cases.
  - Subjective norms are individuals' perceptions of what relevant others would want one to do and one's motivation to comply with those relevant others (Fishbein & Ajzen, 1975).
  - In a meta-analysis, Notani (1998) found that certain behaviors were better predicted by external control, whereas other behaviors were better predicted by internal control.
- These studies suggest that a combination of beliefs, emotions, norms, and self-efficacy determine whether we perform different types of behaviors.

[Transition: Taken together, both uses and gratifications and the TPB may help explain engaging youth in politics.]

Third Main Point: Using Uses and Gratifications and the TPB to Explain Youth Political Engagement

- Section thesis: Motives, emotions, norms, and perceived behavioral control may all explain why some younger people choose to engage in political activities and follow political news while others do not participate.
- Evidence:
  - Delli Carpini (2004) pointed out that both emotions and information determine attitudes toward political engagement, and these are things that people learn beginning in childhood.
  - Lee, Shah, and McLeod (2013) found that peer norms and having political discussions in the classroom can increase political engagement in youth. This speaks to the importance of norms.

STEP 5

    ◦ Also, Lee et al. (2013) found that new media may be a good way to get more young people involved, which fits with previous findings about political efficacy. New media may make young people feel more efficacy. National studies have suggested that young people are likely to get their political information online and that these online activities lead to other types of political participation (Smith, 2013).

- Section conclusion: Forming motives, norms, and efficacy for political engagement happens over the course of a person's lifetime.

Synthesis: Derivation of Hypotheses and Research Questions

- **Synthesis and justification for further research:** In all, research suggests that motives (Palmgreen & Rayburn, 1984), attitudes, norms, perceived behavioral control (Ajzen, 1985), and affect may be good predictors of political engagement through the news and actual political participation (Rivis et al., 2009). Thus, there are clear benefits to further exploring these variables. Also, as Herr (2009) pointed out, it is unclear how affect is related to other variables that predict political behavior.
- **Hypotheses about relationships among variables based on conclusions reached and critique**
  - ◦ **H1:** Motives, attitudes, norms, behavioral control and affect will predict a) political news use and b) political engagement by young people.
  - ◦ **RQ1:** How is affect related to motives, attitudes, norms, and behavioral control in young people?

Conclusion

- **Review:** This paper reviewed different types of media use motives and TPB variables to predict political news use and other types of political engagement in young people.
- **Fulfillment of purpose:** These theories were used to explain how to get more young people involved in politics, particularly through use of early socialization in classrooms, from peers and parents, and through new media.
- **Reiteration:** Clearly affect is an important variable that could add to the discussion about motives, attitudes, norms, and behavioral control. Understanding these variables better and using this research to design political messages may help reach out to and involve younger citizens.

1. Activity: Literature Review Outline Worksheet

Complete this worksheet using full sentences. Provide in-text citations for articles you are using.

Complete the form below to put together an outline for your literature review.

I. **Introduction:**
- Attention-getting statement:
- Thesis:
- Relevance / Importance:
- Preview of main points:

II. **First Main Point:**
- Section thesis:
- Evidence:
- First conclusion:

[**Transition:**   ]

III. **Section 2: Second grouping of related articles from synthesizing worksheet.**
- Section thesis:
- Evidence:
- Second conclusion:

[**Transition:**   ]

IV. **Section 3: Third grouping of related articles from synthesizing worksheet.**
- Section thesis:
- Evidence:
- Third conclusion:

[**Transition:**   ]

V. **Synthesis**
- Synthesis and justification for further research with citations:
- Hypotheses and Research Questions based on synthesis:

VI. **Conclusion**
- Review points:
- Impactful end:

2. Outline Checklist

Trade outlines with a peer in your class. Complete this checklist to assess the thoroughness of his or her outline and have your peer do the same for your outline.

Introduction

___ Attention-getter is interesting and on-topic

___ Thesis is a clear, declarative statement of purpose

___ Clear statement of the importance of the topic

___ Preview reviews all main points, in the order they appear in the paper

Main Points

___ 2–5 clear main points
___ Main points are related to each other
___ Main points are distinct
___ Main points all support the thesis for the paper
___ Main points are well organized
___ Main points include in-text citations to relevant literature in APA format

Transitions

___ There is a transition between each main point
___ There is a transition between the final main point and synthesis

Synthesis

___ Arguments are derived from all of the main points
___ Relevant articles are cited
___ Clearly points to conclusions drawn from the literature
___ Clearly explains areas of ambiguity, uncertainty, or conflict in the literature

Hypotheses / Research Questions

___ First hypothesis / research question is worded clearly
___ First hypothesis / research question is justified by the synthesis
___ Second hypothesis / research question is worded clearly
___ Second hypothesis / research question is justified by the synthesis

Conclusion

___ Clear review of main ideas
___ Meaningful / impactful ending

STEP 6

The Sixth Step in Your Investigation: Write up Your Final Report

Really, the bulk of the case is already complete at this point: You have a clear and focused topic, evidence, and you have organized that evidence in support of specific conclusions. You have detailed notes on the content of the articles from your annotations and you have an outline of where the content of those summaries should go in your paper. Therefore, most of what you're doing in the final stage of writing the paper is editing content that already exists. You should always refer to a writing style guide before writing a final draft of the paper. There, you will find details on language use, citations, references, paper format, paper sections, etc. After going over some tips for integrating your annotations and outline into a final paper, we go over some elements of good writing and cover some highlights of APA style to guide your writing.

As a general rule, all of the content in your paper should follow the three Cs: It should be correct, clear, and concise. **Correct** means that it is accurate, thorough, and adheres to the style guidelines for writing. **Clear** means that it is written in a way that is easy for your reader to understand. **Concise** means that we write in a way that is succinct and to the point.

THIS CHAPTER COVERS:

A. Using Your Outline and Annotations to Write the Paper
B. Defining Concepts and Explaining Theories
C. Grammar and Syntax
   1. Active versus Passive Voice
   2. Avoiding Bias in Language
   3. Parallel Form
   4. Subject-Verb Agreement
   5. Choosing the Correct Words
D. Punctuation
   1. Commas
   2. Colon (:) versus Semicolon (;)
   3. Quotation Marks
   4. Apostrophes
E. Clarity
   1. Parenthetical Elements
   2. Prepositions
   3. Terminology
F. Being Concise
   1. Wordiness
   2. First, Second, and Third Person Pronouns in APA Style

G. Formatting the Paper
   1. Spaces and Spacing
   2. Headings
   3. The Title Page
   4. Running Head and Page Numbers
   5. The Abstract

A. Using Your Outline and Annotations to Write the Paper

There are several mistakes that professors have noted in students' literature reviews. For example, Shon (2012) pointed out three common mistakes:

1. **Excessive quoting**
2. **Failure to compare, contrast, and critique**
3. **Ad nauseum description of one article, then another, then another (he calls this a "beating-one-horse-to-death problem")**

After years of teaching students to write literature reviews and reading their final products, we agree with Shon's conclusions. Fortunately, having annotations that are written in your own words, a chart that compares and contrasts the articles, and sections throughout the literature review that integrate and synthesize your sources will help you avoid these common pitfalls.

You have two options for how to begin writing your paper: Write the complete paper in the outline format then reformat it into a final paper when it is complete, or reformat the outline into a paper and build up each section one-by-one. We recommend the first approach: put the entire paper into the outline, then format it when it's complete.

> **Helpful Tip**
> Write your paper directly into the outline you have already put together. This way, you can be sure that you have all of the elements required for a quality paper (an introduction, clear main points with transitions, a synthesis and conclusion). Formatting the paper is an easy final step to complete once your paper is complete.

© iQoncept, 2014. Shutterstock, Inc.

You may wonder why we recommend this, so we'll give you a few of our many reasons. First, it ensures that the *structure* of the paper remains clear throughout the writing process. Second, it is *easier to "move around"* when writing the paper if it is still in the outline format. Put another way, you can work a little on one main point, then another main point, then go back and reflect those changes in the introduction and conclusion more easily if the paper is still in an outline format with all of the parts clearly labeled. Third, it ensures that all of the essential components of the paper are present in the complete draft. When we start moving content between two documents, such as moving between an outline and a paper, it is easy to forget to transfer something that should be included. Also, when working within the content of the paper itself, we are going to do a lot of moving, deleting, and rewriting. Sometimes, essential elements get deleted and we forget to put them back in the paper. So, just to be safe, it's best to have all of the labeled elements visible while we write.

B. Defining Concepts and Explaining Theories

The first element that we should look at in our outlines is the key concepts and / or theories we discuss. We should note each concept and theory that we refer to in our outline, and give a definition or explanation of those before we get into discussing the research. Clear definitions and consistent use of the names of specific theories and concepts throughout your paper are essential for clear writing. Therefore, always define concepts clearly before discussing them; be consistent in how you label them; and only abbreviate variable names when necessary and after writing out the full variable or theory name.

For example, in a paper about CMC, I would state the definition and provide the acronym early in my paper: "*Computer-mediated communication (CMC) is communication between people that occurs via some mediated channel, which includes computers and cellphones.*" Once this variable is defined and the abbreviation is explained, every time I write "CMC" my reader will know exactly what I'm talking about. If I were to call it something else (like starting to talk about communication via new media), or stop using the abbreviation, it may confuse readers. The key is to be consistent.

Similarly, when we introduce a theory, we need to explain that theory: the key concepts, how they are related to each other, and the typical applications of that theory. If we are using one theory throughout our paper, then it is preferable to begin the paper with an overview of the theory. If we are discussing different theories in different main points, then we begin each main point with an explanation of the theory discussed in that main point.

C. Grammar and Syntax

While organization, definitions, and explanations are important macro-level writing guidelines, there are many micro-level issues that will also affect the clarity of our writing. The first issue to address is grammar. **Grammar** is how words are used to make sentences, and it includes syntax (The Free Dictionary, 2014a). **Syntax** is the rules we follow to form sentences and phrases (The Free Dictionary, 2014b).

Yoda is probably the best example of bad grammar and syntax. Consider this quote from Yoda: "Size matters not. Look at me. Judge me by my size, do you? Hmm? Hmm. And well you should not. For my ally is the Force, and a powerful ally it is."

Imagine if Yoda said this instead: "Size does not matter. Look at me. Do you judge me by my size? Hmm? You should not. For my ally is the force, and it is a powerful ally." Granted, his character would be less endearing. But he would have been much clearer if he had better grammar and syntax. There are 5 common grammar and syntax rules that are often violated in students' writing: using active voice, avoiding biased language, having parallel form in lists, subject-verb agreement, and choosing the correct words.

1. Active versus Passive Voice

One of the issues with Yoda's speaking pattern is that he uses passive voice. We use active voice for professional writing because it is clearer. Also, APA recommends writing in active voice. Active voice helps writers avoid common grammar mistakes, like dangling modifiers and sentence fragments. **Active voice** sentences have a **subject** *then* a **verb**. The subject *does* the action. The verb *is* the action. A complete sentence has both a subject and a verb. Sentences that are missing either a subject or a verb are **fragments**.

Active voice (correct):
The researchers tested the hypothesis.
     ^   ^
   subject   verb

Passive voice (incorrect):
The hypothesis was tested by the researchers.
            ^   ^
           verb   subject

Fragment (incorrect; no verb):
Researchers' hypothesis tests.

Fragment (incorrect; no subject):
Not supported.

Long fragment (incorrect; no verb in the independent clause):
The researchers' hypothesis, that there is a relationship between two things, which modified the relationship between those things, not supported.

Learn more about active voice here:
http://owl.english.purdue.edu/owl/resource/539/1/

Active voice

Active and passive voice can be difficult to identify, particularly in our own writing. We often speak in passive voice, and passive voice isn't technically grammatically incorrect. Therefore passive voice is an easy thing to miss when we edit our own work. This is also true of bias in language—it is very subtle, technically grammatically correct, but does not meet APA standards.

2. Avoiding Bias in Language

As communication scholars, we are keenly aware of how language impacts people's thoughts and behaviors. Therefore, we have to be very careful about how we talk *to* other people and *about* people. Here are the APA's guidelines for reducing bias in language:

1. *Gender* does not refer to biological sex; it refers to a cultural definition of gender types. *Sex* refers to biological sex.
2. *Avoid labeling groups of people*, or discussing groups of people in ways that imply judgment or evaluation. Rather than writing, "gays had different relationship expectations compared to straight men," we would write "men who were gay reported different relationship expectations compared to men who were heterosexual." Similarly, we avoid labeling groups of people based on their disability status. For example, rather than writing "autistic children" we would write "children with autism."
3. *Be clear about the group of people being discussed.* If you are looking at "adolescents" define what you mean by that. Similarly, be clear about the racial and ethnic groups that you discuss, but do so using the "commonly accepted designations" for those groups (APA, p. 75).
4. *Do not use the generic "he" or generic "man"* unless you are talking about a study that only included men. Therefore, titles like police*man*, congress*man*, chair*man*, etc. should be police officer, congressional representative, and chairperson.

Many people dismiss guidelines like these as being overly sensitive or forcing political correctness. Bear in mind, though, that we write our papers with the expectation that we will have a large, diverse audience and that this audience may span years, or even decades. So we need to write in a way that is least likely to offend a broad audience and will avoid the possibility that, in 30 years, someone will read our paper and think that we're racist, sexist, or homophobic.

3. Parallel Form

All items in a list should be in the same tense. This is called **parallel form**. It is unclear and awkward to read writing that fails to conform to the rules of parallel form. Tense can be confusing: When is something past, present, or future tense? As a general guideline, regardless of which tense you use, you should use it consistently. If you are going to write in past tense when discussing research that has been conducted, then every article you discuss should be talked about in the past tense. This rule is particularly true in terms of writing sentences and paragraphs. Within a list in a sentence, all elements in the list must be in the same tense.

Parallel Form (correct):
We stud**ied** it, **found** no support, and chang**ed** our approach.
          past tense past tense   past tense

Parallel Form (correct):
We will be read**ing**, writ**ing**, and edit**ing** our own work.
          future tense   future tense   future tense

Parallel Form (incorrect):
We stud**ied** it, **find** no support, and it chang**es** our approach.
          past tense present tense   present tense

Tenses

Learn more about tenses here: http://leo.stcloudstate.edu/grammar/tenses.html

4. Subject-Verb Agreement

The subject, verb, and object in a sentence should all be in agreement. This can be tricky, but as a rule of thumb, if the subject of the sentence can be counted or represents many, we use the plural forms of verbs. If the subject is singular, we use the singular form of verbs.

Agreement (correct):
The researcher**s** **have** agreed.
    plural subject   plural verb

The **researcher** **has** agreed.
    singular subject singular verb

Three research**ers** **have** agreed.
    plural subject   plural verb

Researcher one **and** researcher two **have** agreed.
          plural subject   plural verb

Agreement (incorrect)
Research have agreed on this conclusion.
    Singular Plural

Subject/verb agreement

Learn more about subject and verb agreement here: http://www.grammarbook.com/grammar/subjectVerbAgree.asp

5. Choosing the Correct Words

There are many reasons for the confusion we often face about how and when to use certain words and whether one word is truly a synonym that can be used to replace another word. One reason for our confusion is the prevalence of homophones in the English language, or words that sound similar but have different meanings. There are also words that are simply confusing due to the complex rules for when you use one word, such as "who," versus another word, such as "whom."

Helpful hint

A good rule of thumb is to look up words if you aren't 100% sure which word to use. There are many online resources for definitions (www.dictionary.com), finding appropriate synonyms (www.thesaurus.com), and deciding between homophones (Purdue OWL's Homophone List: https://owl.english.purdue.edu/engagement/2/1/48/) and homonyms (http://www.grammarbook.com/homonyms/confusing-words-letter-a.asp). If the technical, nitpicky details get to be overwhelming, you can also look at the Oatmeal's humorous explanations of often violated grammar rules: http://theoatmeal.com/tag/grammar.

© doomu, 2014, Shutterstock, Inc.

| dictionary.com | thesaurus.com | Purdue | Confusing words | Oatmeal |

Choosing Correct Words
Commonly Confused Words: A Cheat Sheet

Which	You can omit this from a sentence without changing the meaning. *Ex: This book reviews basic grammar, which is an essential writing skill.*
That	You have to have this in the sentence for it to make sense. *Ex: Papers that do not follow basic grammar rules are less successful.*
It's	This means "it is" or "it has." *Ex: It's difficult to remember all of these grammar and punctuation rules.*
Its	The possessive form of "it." *Ex: The research is clear in its meaning.* Common mistake: Using "it's" as a possessive form of "it."

(continued)

Choosing Correct Words
Commonly Confused Words: A Cheat Sheet (continued)

Who	Used as the subject in the sentence. *Ex: Students who learn about grammar write well.*
Whom	Used as the object in the sentence. *Ex: Whom are professors more likely to pass? Those who can write well!*
Onto	Refers to a position, such as on top of or upon. *Ex: I put your paper onto my stack of grading.*
On to	Does not refer to a position, but may refer to movement toward something. *Ex: In the next section, we move on to punctuation.*
Affect	A verb that means "to influence." *Ex. Grammar affects grades.* A noun that means "experience of emotion." *Ex. Robots do not show affect.*
Effect	Means "to cause" and is also used when explaining a result. *Ex. Grammar has an effect on grades.*
Can	Means that you are able to do something. *Ex. You can find resources online to help with your writing.*
May	Means that you have permission to do something. *Ex. You may use your university's computers to look up these rules.*
Passed	A past tense of the verb "pass." *Ex. I passed the class with flying colors.*
Past	A point in time, location, or used to mean "after." *Ex. I bet you thought that grammar and punctuation lessons were a thing of the past.*
Their	The possessive form of "they." *Ex. The researchers explained their conclusions.* Common mistake: One student had trouble with their paper.
They're	The shortened form of "they are." *Ex. They're going to do fine on their final papers.*
There	A place. *Ex. Turn in your paper over there.*
His or Her	Used to show possession when the subject of the sentence is singular. *Ex. A student forgot his or her book.*

D. Punctuation

1. Commas

Commas can be confusing, because people tend to use them whenever there is any change in a sentence. There are many uses for commas, which increases confusion. Here are a few quick rules for when to use a comma:

1. Use a comma after the introduction to a sentence.
   Ex. First, we will discuss punctuation.
   Ex. There are many things to discuss, beginning with basic grammar and punctuation.

2. Use a comma when there is a clause in the sentence that could be removed without changing the meaning of a sentence.
Ex. Students find writing difficult, even impossible, when they haven't had a quick brush-up on the rules.

3. Use a comma when you have a list of items in a sentence.
Ex. We will cover the rules of grammar, syntax, voice, and punctuation.

4. Use a comma before and after inserting a quotation in the sentence.
Ex. Students said, "I am glad you reminded me of these rules," and thanked me for my time.

5. Use a comma before a contrasting element or afterthought at the end of your sentence.
Ex. Good writing is the key to professional success, but it is not easy to learn.

Here is a good resource about when you should use a comma:
http://grammar.ccc.commnet.edu/grammar/commas.htm#parenthetical

Commas

Common Mistake
Do not use commas mindlessly throughout your paper. Always stop and ask yourself: Is it an introductory element, quote, removable clause, list, or contrasting element? If not, then a comma probably isn't necessary.

© Thomas Bethge, 2014. Shutterstock, Inc.

2. Colon (:) versus Semicolon (;)

Much like commas, there are several reasons for using a colon and a semicolon when you write.

- We use a colon when we have a complete sentence that introduces a list.
Ex. There are two times that you can use a semicolon in a sentence: when you have a complete sentence followed by a list, or when you have a complete sentence followed by a rule or example.

- A semicolon, on the other hand, is used to join together two complete sentences without using a conjunction such as "and, or, but" etc.
Ex: Semicolons are often confused with colons; however, they are not interchangeable.

- Semicolons are also used when you have items in a list and the elements in the list contain commas.
  Ex: There are many professors who teach this material: Dr. Smith, Associate Professor; Dr. Anderson, Full Professor; and Dr. Miller, Chair and Professor.

Here is a good overview of when you use a semicolon (;) versus a colon (:): http://leo.stcloudstate.edu/punct/col-semi.html

Colon Vs.
Semicolon

Tips for success

Many editors do not like colons and semicolons, particularly in APA papers. Typically, a colon or semicolon (except when used to separate items in a list) can be removed and you can have two clear, succinct sentences instead.

© iQoncept, 2014. Shutterstock, Inc.

3. Quotation Marks

There are entire websites devoted to the misuse of quotation marks. People often use them to indicate emphasis, but that is not their purpose. In APA format, we use italics for emphasis. Quotation marks are *only* used for quotations, and there is always punctuation that marks the beginning of a quote contained within a sentence and at the end of the quote. If a quote is contained within a sentence, we use a comma before and at the end of the quote. If a quote is at the end of the sentence, we end the quote with a period or question mark where appropriate.

Periods and commas at the ends of quotations always go inside the quotation mark, but question marks are different. If a quoted question is part of a declarative sentence in your paper, then the question mark goes within the quotation marks.

Ex: My students ask, "Why do we have to learn this?" while they shake their heads.

On the other hand, question marks go outside the quotation marks when the entire sentence is a question that happens to contain a quote.

Ex: Why would a student say, "There is no reason to relearn this material"?

See   http://www.grammarbook.com/punctuation/quotes.asp   for help with punctuation within quotation marks.

Quotation marks

Common Mistake

Do not use quotation marks to emphasize words. Use italics.

In APA format, we do not use quotation marks around the titles of books, movies, or TV shows. We italicize those titles when discussing them in our papers.

© Thomas Bethge, 2014, Shutterstock, Inc.

4. Apostrophes

Many people struggle with when to use an apostrophe. Here are a few quick tips to decide if you should use an apostrophe and, if so, where to put it.

Use:	's	s'	No apostrophe	As a Replacement
Example:	The student**'s** paper is complete.	My student**s'** papers are complete.	My class finished **its** assignment.	My students in the '90s didn't like punctuation rules either.
Rule:	Use an apostrophe *before* an s when the word is singular (or plural, but does not end in s) and you are showing possession.	Use an apostrophe *after* the s when the word ends in s, including when the word ends in s to make a plural form. If the word is already plural without having to add an s (such as women, children, men, etc.), we do not use an apostrophe after the s.	We do not use an apostrophe to make it a possessive form. There is also no apostrophe when we add an s to the end of the word to make a plural, non-possessive form (e.g., "I have students").	Apostrophes are used when we form contractions (e.g., "it's" meaning "it is"). They signify that part of the word or phrase is missing. **We do not use contractions in formal writing.** Apostrophes are also used when we shorten a year (e.g., from 1990s to '90s).

E. Clarity

Sentences can be grammatically correct, but may still be difficult to understand or just plain awkward to read. Three common errors are unnecessary interjections, ending sentences with prepositional phrases, and confusing terminology.

STEP 6

1. Parenthetical Elements

Avoid unnecessary parenthetical elements in sentences. Parenthetical elements interrupt a sentence. For example, this sentence has a parenthetical element: "There are too many grammar rules, many of them arcane, to teach all of them." In this example sentence, "many of them arcane" is a parenthetical element. As in this example, parenthetical elements are interjected into the sentence using a comma or dash at the beginning and end of the interjection. This interrupts the "complete thought" in the sentence. It is clearer to write: "Many grammar rules are arcane. Therefore we will not teach all of them."

2. Prepositions

Writers should also avoid ending sentences in prepositional phrases. **Prepositions** are words that explain a type of relationship. Common prepositions include with, of, for, by, as, in, on, etc. It is generally ok to end a sentence with a prepositional phrase if changing the sentence would make it wordier.

For example:

Correct use of a preposition:
Many scholars agree with this conclusion.
                        ^
                   preposition

Awkward use of a preposition:
The conclusion is one that many scholars agree with.
                                              ^
                                         preposition

Learn more about prepositional phrases here:
http://grammar.yourdictionary.com/parts-of-speech/prepositions/
Ending-a-Sentence-with-a-Preposition.html

Prepositions

3. Terminology

In addition to the rules about grammar, voice, and syntax, we also have to be careful of the terminology we use when we write. Writing in the social sciences and about academic research is a balancing act: we need people to understand what we mean, but we also want to adhere to the conventions of our discipline. An important rule of thumb is to use only the jargon you have to use to be *accurate*, and do not replace jargon with colloquial expressions.

Jargon. The APA recommends that writers avoid colloquial expressions and unnecessary jargon. In the social sciences, our writing is often full of jargon, and we go over some of this technical vocabulary in Step 2 and Step 5. Because of the technical nature of academic research, some jargon is necessary, such as using the exact names of variables, specific names of theories, and exact names of statistical tests. That being said, we should not introduce any unnecessary jargon that would make our paper even more difficult to read.

The key to using jargon effectively is to provide *definitions* and to be *consistent*. If we are referring to sitcoms, we would not refer to them as "primetime family comedy programs" because that is wordy and introduces even more jargon into our writing. It sounds repetitive, but it is clearer to refer to them simply as "sitcoms" throughout our paper, from beginning to end. As a general rule of thumb, only use the jargon that is necessary given the scope and purpose of your paper. Also, when we first talk about "sitcoms" in our paper, we should explain to our reader what we mean when we use that term by providing a clear, research-based definition of "sitcom" programs.

Colloquial expressions. Colloquial expressions include substituting a word or phrase for a more commonly used phrase or using generalities when specifics are in order (APA, 2009). People often use colloquial expressions to make their writing less formal and more approachable to readers. But we have to be careful about the precision of our expression. For example, in formal writing, we refer to "television" or "TV" rather than "the idiot box" or the "boob tube."

Example of too much jargon: "The dyadic partners' mean scores in perceived homophily were significantly improved by mediated disclosure."

Example of being too colloquial: "People were more into each other when they shared secrets online."

Best of the two extremes: "Couples felt more homophily when they self-disclosed online. Homophily is perceived similarity between two people."

F. Being Concise

1. Wordiness

In addition to carefully balancing the need to be accurate and understandable, writers also have to be careful about wordiness. **Wordiness** is when we use more words than we need to use to convey our meaning. We can be more succinct by replacing common phrases with single words that have the exact same meaning. Check out Purdue's list of wordy phrases and replacements: http://owl.english.purdue.edu/owl/resource/572/04/.

Scan this code to visit the Purdue Online Writing Lab's list of replacement words to help your writing be more concise.

Example of excessive wordiness: "On the occasions that people interact online it is important that they be honest in light of the fact that they may meet face-to-face."

There are several wordy phrases used in this sentence that don't really add much important information: "on the occasions" and "it is important that" are unnecessary.

STEP 6

Better, less wordy alternative: "When people interact online they should be honest because they might meet face-to-face."

Helpful Tip

Not sure about your grammar? Paste your text into Grammerly.com for a review: http://www.grammarly.com/?q=grammar&gclid=CNnF2qSaqrYCFa9aMgod-R8A7Q

---

2. First, Second, and Third Person Pronouns in APA Style

Part of the awkwardness that is often present in students' early academic writing is that we have to avoid use of first and second person in APA writing. APA suggests that writers avoid first person pronouns (I, me, my, our, we, us) unless those pronouns are absolutely necessary. *Do not* use second person pronouns in APA (you, your). When discussing researchers, research participants, or populations, *use third person pronouns* (they, their, him, her, or a non-inflammatory label, like "students" or "participants").

First Person:
I am going to explain three elements of good writing.
First person pronouns include: I, me, my, we, our, us

Second Person:
You will understand the three elements of good writing.
Second person pronouns include: you, your

Third Person:
They will understand the three elements of good writing.
Third person pronouns include: him, her, they, them, their

That being said, it is also awkward to use "This paper" in place of a pronoun, as in, "*This paper reviews* common grammatical mistakes." It is clearer to write, "*I will review* common grammatical mistakes." So, in those cases, first person pronouns are acceptable.

G. Formatting the Paper

Once we have written the paper using the outline, we are ready to format it to conform to APA standards. In general, your paper should conform to the following rules:

- Use a legible font, such as Times, Arial, or Cambria.
- Have 1" margins for the entire paper
- Never contain any underlining
- Everything is double-spaced
- The beginning of each paragraph is tabbed in five spaces
- Use headings for major sections to guide your reader
- Have a title page
- Have headings and page numbers on every page

1. Spaces and Spacing

Double-spacing. If your outline isn't double-spaced, then select everything in your document—yes, *everything*—and double-space it. Everything on the title page, throughout the entire paper, and in the reference list is double-spaced.

After everything is double-spaced there is no need to add any additional spaces after paragraphs or sections. There are no extra spaces between sections of the paper, paragraphs, or references. The only exception to this rule is when we use a page break to avoid having a header for a section at the very bottom of a page (i.e., a dangling header).

Periods. There are two spaces after every period in the abstract and body of the paper. There is only one space after periods in the references.

Page breaks. There are three page breaks in the paper:

- The title page is on its own page, so there is a page break at the end of the title page.
- The abstract is on its own page, so there is a page break after the last line of the abstract. The paper begins on the next page.
- The references begin on a new page, so there is a page break after the last line of the paper.

2. Headings

Think of headings as a visual guide that your reader can use to quickly see the most important sections of your paper. The number and type of headers you use will depend on how long your paper is, how many main points you cover, and how developed the sub-points are for each main point.

The key to using headings effectively throughout the paper is to be consistent and follow the principle of subordination. Your paper is a hierarchy of ideas: from your general purpose (the thesis statement), to the main points, to the supporting evidence within each main point. First-level headings are used for general sections of the paper, such as the body of the paper and conclusion. Second-level headings are used for more specific main points within each general section. If we are writing a very long and detailed analysis of the literature, then we would use third-level headings to label the very specific areas of research within each main point. So headings, like the organization of main points, go from *general, overarching headings*, to more *specific subject headings*, to *very specific concept headings*.

1. A general, Level 1 heading is centered, capitalized, and bold. There is a hard return, then you start a paragraph on the next line. First-level headings are useful for labeling the major sections of your paper (Literature Review, Hypotheses, Conclusion).
2. A more specific, Level 2 heading is left justified, capitalized, and bold. There is a hard return, then you start the paragraph on the next line. Second-level headings are useful for labeling the main points in your paper.
3. A Level 3 heading is indented, bold, lowercase, and has a period at the end. There are two spaces, then you start the paragraph on the same line as the heading. Third-level headings are useful for the sub-topics within each main point.

For example, this is how first-, second-, and third-level headings would *look* for a paper with four primary sections (Introduction, Body, Hypotheses, and Conclusion), two main points, and two important concepts discussed in each main point.

Introduction

Body

Main Point 1

    Concept one.

    Concept two.

Main Point 2

    Concept one.

    Concept two.

Hypotheses and Research Questions

Conclusion

Headings throughout the paper should clearly reflect the specific content of the section we are labeling. If we are talking about a group of related concepts, our heading should reflect how those concepts are related. If we are talking about a particular theory in the section being labeled, then the theory should be part of our heading.

The most important rule for using headings throughout the paper is to use them consistently. If you have a heading for the first main point, you need to use the same level of heading for every subsequent main point. Headings can help guide your reader through the main points in your paper, signal to your reader that topics are changing, and also ensure that you organize your ideas into logical groupings and make a coherent argument in your paper. But these benefits are only possible when headings are used consistently throughout the entire paper.

For clarity, if you have hypotheses and research questions, you should also label those.

- Label each hypothesis with an H and number them consecutively, as in: H1, H2, H3, etc.
- Label each research question with an RQ, and number them consecutively but separately from the hypotheses, as in: RQ1, RQ2, RQ3, etc.
- Tab hypotheses in five spaces, so they look like a block quote and stand out from the written text.

Helpful tip

Use the parts of your outline to create headings for your paper. Look at each main point in the outline and give it a heading that reflects the content of that main point. These become second-level headings. If your supporting evidence within each main point can be grouped together into coherent sub-points, you could even label those. Those sub-points would get third-level headings.

© iQoncept, 2014. Shutterstock, Inc.

3. The Title Page

The title page has three elements that are centered on the first page:

- The title of your paper
- Your name
- Your institution (or course name)

The title of your paper should be brief, incorporate the most relevant concepts in your paper, and generally indicate the goal or purpose of your paper. APA guidelines suggest that the title be approximately 12 words and it should be in plain text. Titles do not need to be complete sentences, and should also not be generic titles reflecting the assignment (i.e., "My Final Paper"). Your full name is on the line after the title, and the last line on the title page is your institution (or course).

If you plan to submit this paper to a conference, you can also include an "Author Note" that gives your title and contact information. If you choose to do this, you center "Author Note" on the page, and then any information you want to or are required to include is in paragraph format, left justified, in plain text under the heading.

The entire title page is double-spaced and there is a page number in the upper right-hand corner of the page. The title page is always page 1.

4. Running Head and Page Numbers

The title page and every page of the paper should have a running head and page number. The running head is a brief form of your title. The running head is labeled "**Running head**" on the title page and the label is bold, then just the running head itself appears on each subsequent page.

To insert a page number in Microsoft Word®, click on "Insert" then select "page numbers." The position of the page number should be "top of the page" and the alignment should be "right."

Once the page numbers are inserted, you need to insert your running head on page 1. The running head is aligned with the page number in the header (the top margin) of the document.

1. Double click inside the header (the top margin of the paper)
2. Type **Running head:**
3. Type your complete running head, in all capital letters
4. Left justify the running head (if it doesn't default to left justified)

The running head on the first page is different from the running head used throughout the rest of the paper because on the first page it is labeled "Running head." To use the required, different running head on subsequent pages:

1. Click on "Header and Footer" in the Word® toolbar while the header is highlighted.
2. Check the box next to the option "Different first page"
3. Scroll to the second page
4. Put the running head, without the bolded label, in the second page header

5. The Abstract

The abstract is on the second page of the paper. It is labeled "Abstract" (centered on the first line of the page, capitalized, but not bolded or italicized). An abstract is a brief, approximately 100 to 150-word summary of your paper.

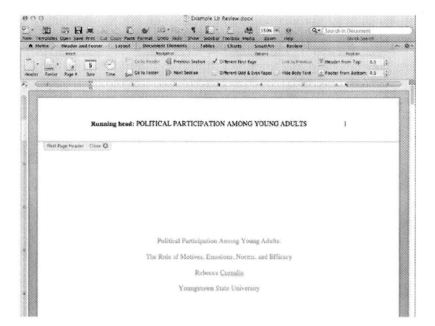

Under the abstract, we have a list of keywords that are used to index our paper. Write "*Keywords*" (capitalized, in italics, followed by a colon, and centered on the page), then list a few of the key concepts in your paper.

Here is an example abstract page:

POLITICAL PARTICIPATION AMONG YOUNG ADULTS   2

Abstract

This paper is a review of the different reasons people follow political news from the uses and gratifications perspective and the different variables that affect political participation from the theory of planned behavior. Motives, beliefs, emotions, peer norms, and having a sense of efficacy are discussed as determinants of political engagement. These variables are considered in light of political engagement via new media, which may increase young people's involvement in politics by satisfying their motives, promoting favorable beliefs, and increasing a sense of normative pressure and efficacy.

Keywords: political participation, voting, motives, Theory of Planned Behavior

REFERENCES

American Psychological Association. (2009). *Publication manual of the American Psycho-logical Association* (6th ed.). Washington, DC: American Psychological Association.

The Free Dictionary. (2014a) Grammar. Retrieved from http://www.thefreedictionary.com/grammar

The Free Dictionary. (2014b) Syntax. Retrieved from http://www.thefreedictionary.com/syntax

Shon, P. C. H. (2012). *How to read journal articles in the social sciences: A very practical guide for students.* Los Angeles: Sage.

Example Literature Review

Political Participation Among Young Adults:

Understanding Their Motives, Emotions, Norms, and Efficacy

Rebecca Curnalia

Youngstown State University

Author Note:

Rebecca Curnalia, Ph.D., is an Associate Professor in the Department of Communication at Youngstown State University where she teaches communication theory, research methods, and senior capstone courses. This paper is an example of what she expects to see in her undergraduate students' senior capstones. She can be reached via email at rmcurnalia@ysu.edu.

Notice that I have a title that reviews all of the major concepts in my paper

My name

Where I am from

STEP 6

This is labeled "Abstract"

Notice that the first line of the abstract *is not* indented.

My abstract is 87 words, and clearly summarizes all of the main points and my overarching conclusion.

Notice that my key words are labeled, and that they are the exact concepts that are the main points in my paper

Abstract

This paper is a review of the different reasons people follow political news from the uses and gratifications perspective and the different variables that affect political participation from the theory of planned behavior. Motives, beliefs, emotions, peer norms, and having a sense of efficacy are discussed as determinants of political engagement. These variables are considered in light of political engagement via new media, which may increase young people's involvement in politics by satisfying their motives, promoting favorable beliefs, and increasing a sense of normative pressure and efficacy.

Keywords: political participation, youth, Uses and Gratifications, Theory of Planned Behavior

Political Participation Among Young Adults: The Role of Motives,
Emotions, Norms, and Efficacy

In 2012, only 41% of voters age 18 to 24 voted in the presidential election (Taylor & Lopez, 2013). Many researchers and politicians are concerned that younger people do not follow politics and are not politically active. This paper is a review of the research on political activity to explore some of the reasons people are more or less likely to be engaged in American politics. By better understanding how and why people follow politics, researchers will be able to make recommendations about how to get more people interested and, hopefully, get more people voting in elections. Two theories are discussed that help explain how and why people follow the news and participate in politics: uses and gratifications, which explains motives for news use, and the theory of planned behavior (TPB).

Uses and Gratifications and the Theory of Planned Behavior

The first concern when considering how best to get young people involved in politics is how to inform them. One perspective that may help with this is uses and gratifications, which explains the reasons that people use different types of media to fulfill their needs (Palmgreen, 1984). Understanding motives may help researchers and practitioners understand how best to reach younger voters.

Motives for Political News Use

There are different types of motives for media use identified in news research. or example, Greenberg (1974) used open-ended questions to create a typology of television viewing motives for British children. Eight viewing motives were identified: passing time, diversion, to learn about the world, to learn about oneself, for arousal, relaxation, companionship, and habit. People use different types of media to find out about who they are or who they could be. People also seek out emotional stimulation, or sometimes use media just to relax or take a break. Media is also used as an alternative to having face-to-face interactions, or even for conversational topics in people's 'real' relationships. Lastly, there are a lot of media that people use as part of their daily routines.

Rubin (1984) identified ritualistic and instrumental motives from a typology that was similar to Greenberg's (1974). Ritualistic motives include using

---

Margin notes:

The attention-getter is a good opportunity to find some interesting statistics related to your topic.

This is a first level header because it is one of the main sections in my paper.

Notice that I am defining concepts as I discuss them in the paper.

Notice how this thesis statement relates back to the problem question posed at the very beginning of this book: "How can we get more people involved in politics?"

I use a colon here because I have a complete thought, "Two theories are discussed that help explain how and why people follow the news and participate in politics," that introduces a list.

This is a second level header, because it is an important main point within this section.

STEP 6

the media for more habitual reasons. The motives are less active and pur-posive. This includes using media to relax and out of habit. Instrumental motives are more active and intentional, and this includes those motives that are centered on being informed, developing conversational topics, and man-aging moods. So, Greenberg's typology has held up in subsequent research, but it has two distinct dimensions.

Motives are important because they affect which forms of media people select and how they interact with that media (Perse, 1992). People with active motives pay closer attention and think more carefully about news content, which is called involvement. Using items similar to Rubin (1984) and Perse (1992), Rayburn and Palmgreen (1984) looked at keeping up with issues, finding out about officials, entertainment, supporting one's viewpoints to others, news casters' human quality, sharing information with others, drama, comparing one's own ideas, conversational topics, excitement, reporters being like others one knows, making up one's mind, trustworthy information, and finding out about issues that may affect one's self. These motives were related to whether people used the news. Interestingly, Palmgreen (1984) makes the point that the important contribution of uses and gratifications theory is the emphasis it places on expectations. Specifically, people's expectations about what they will get out of a particular type of media content influences whether they use that content and how they use it.

After reviewing the different types of motives for news use introduced by Greenberg (1974), Rubin (1984), Perse (1992), and Rayburn and Palmgreen (1984), one thing is clear: motives are either active reasons for using the news or passive, diversionary reasons. They include a combination of cognitive and affective reasons for using news media. Therefore, motives likely predict one type of political behavior: following politics in the news. Understanding the media that young people are using, how they use it, and why they use it could help get them involved in politics, as campaigns and the news media could create and disseminate media content that appeals to younger people's motives and disseminate that content through media channels that young people are likely to use.

For example, Pew Research (2012) found that young people were get-ting political news from websites, and more young people used Facebook and Twitter to get their news compared to people 30 years old and older. Facebook was a particularly important source of political information for younger people. Therefore, to reach those young people, practitioners need to understand why they are using Facebook and other online sources to then match those needs.

This is a good example of integrating sources: point-ing out how they are similar and different. These points of comparison and contrast should be evident after you complete your analysis of your sources and identify trends and themes.

POLITICAL PARTICIPATION AMONG YOUNG ADULTS   5

Theory of Planned Behavior

Motives affect what we watch, read, and listen to, and the TPB predicts what we do. Ajzen (1985) introduced the TPB to explain how individuals' attitudes are related to their behavior. According to the TPB, people's intentions to perform a behavior such as watching the news are the result of three individual judgments: (a) Attitude toward the behavior, including beliefs about the expected outcomes of the behavior and the strength of beliefs; (b) norms for the behavior and motivation to comply with that normative pressure; and (c) the perception that one is able to perform the behavior, or has behavioral control.

Each person holds a lot of different beliefs in memory for a lot of different behaviors. These beliefs vary in favorability (Durnan & Trafimow, 2000). People may have a combination of positive, neutral, and negative beliefs in memory for any given behavior, including political activity. When a negative belief is activated, other associated negative beliefs are also activated in memory. Beliefs have both affective (evaluative) and cognitive (informational) aspects (Lavine, Thomsen, Zanna, & Borgida, 1998). So, when determining a belief about a topic such as politics, people will consider both their feelings about politics and the information that they have stored in memory about politics.

In terms of political activity, people's emotions may be an important determinant of whether involvement in politics is perceived as valuable and worthwhile. Rivis, Sheeran, and Armitage (2009) and Herr (1995) said that affect is an important part of predicting behavior in addition to beliefs, norms, and perceived behavioral control. In reviewing the literature on the TPB, it was clear that emotions play a significant role in whether or not people perform a lot of different types of behaviors, though there is still some debate about whether or not emotions should be included in the TPB.

Lavine et al. (1998) also found that affect may be more important than cognitive beliefs in some cases. When emotions and information are contradictory, people tend to vote according to their feelings. This has important implications for understanding political activity because people may have the information they need about voting, such as how, when, where, and why they should participate in politics, but they may also have negative feelings about the political process in America. These negative feelings may deter them from participation.

In addition to beliefs and emotions, feeling normative pressure to do something also increases behavior. Subjective norms are individuals' perceptions of what relevant others would want one to do and one's motivation to comply with those relevant others (Fishbein & Ajzen, 1975). Norms

---

Notice that, even though there is a header, there is still a transition that links these two main points together.

Because there are three or more authors, and I have already cited all of them, I use "et al." from this point forward in the paper.

The second level heading marks my shift to the second main point in this section.

STEP 6

motivate people to do things. Therefore, political norms within a person's social group or family may influence the likelihood of him or her being motivated to participate in politics.

Even when attitudes are positive and norms are in favor of a behavior, people still may not perform the desired behavior. To choose to perform a behavior, a person has to feel a sense of efficacy, or perceived behavioral control. In a meta-analysis, Notani (1998) found that certain behaviors were better predicted by external control, whereas other behaviors were better predicted by internal control. External control includes barriers to performing a behavior that exist in the situation or environment. Things like lack of transportation, not knowing where to go to vote, or not know how to become active in politics in one's area are external barriers to political participation. On the other hand, a person may feel that they do not have enough information or do not understand the process, and this may lead them to avoid politics due to a reduced sense of internal control. Therefore, in addition to attitudes and norms, political practitioners must be concerned about enabling people to participate.

These studies suggest that a combination of beliefs, emotions, norms, and self-efficacy determine whether people perform different types of behaviors. The TPB may be explain why people participate in or avoid politics by clarifying that a person must have positive attitudes that are a combination of positive feelings and information, normative pressure to participate, and a sense that he or she is able to participate. Taken together with the findings on motives, both uses and gratifications and the TPB may help explain how to engage youth in politics.

> This is the second section of my paper, where I bring it all together

Using Uses and Gratifications and the TPB to Explain Youth Political Engagement

Motives, emotions, norms, and perceived behavioral control may all explain why younger people choose to engage in political activities and follow political news while others do not participate. In keeping with the conclusions made about using the TPB to predict behavior, research in political activity has suggested that both information and emotion are important determinants of political activity.

Instilling Motivation, Norms, and Efficacy

For example, Delli Carpiini (2004) pointed out that both emotions and information determine attitudes toward political engagement, and these are things that people learn beginning in childhood. Political engagement is a

POLITICAL PARTICIPATION AMONG YOUNG ADULTS   6

combination of being interested in political information, such as news, partic- ← *I'm using a semicolon because these are items in a list and the first item includes a comma.*
ipating in political discussions; and participating in political activities. School
debates and interactions with peers and parents in one's youth can help shape
positive beliefs about political activity from a young age. Further, these activities may promote a sense of efficacy and reinforce normative pressure to be
involved in politics as well. In terms of research that supports this explanation, Lee, Shah, and McLeod (2013) found that peer norms and having political discussions in the classroom increase political engagement in youth. This
speaks to the importance of norms, just as the TPB would predict.

In addition to classroom discussions, reaching young people via new media
may be an important means of getting them involved in politics. Lee et al.
(2013) found that new media may be a good way to get more young people
involved, which fits with previous findings about political efficacy. New media
may make young people feel more efficacy because it is a familiar and comfortable channel for them where political information can be delivered and
discussed. Thinking about these results from a uses and gratifications perspective, connecting with younger potential voters via social media, which they
use for many complex reasons and in many ways, may prove to be a great
way to improve enjoyment, involvement and engagement in politics. A recent
Pew study of political participation suggested that most young people get their
political information online, and getting that online information lead to other
types of political participation (Smith, 2013).

Forming prosocial motives, norms, and a sense of efficacy for political
engagement happens over the course of a person's lifetime, and begins at a
young age. Clearly, the goal of getting more young people involved in politics
involves reaching them via formats that they are comfortable with and that
they enjoy.

Derivation of Hypotheses and Research Questions

I justify my hy- potheses based on the lit- erature I have cited. →
In all, research suggests that motives (Rayburn & Palmgreen, 1984),
attitudes, norms, perceived behavioral control (Ajzen, 1985), and emotion
(Herr, 1995) may determine political engagement through the news and
actual political participation (Rivis et al., 2009). Thus, there are clear benefits
to further exploring these variables to help understand why some young people engage in political activity while other young people do not participate.

I specify how I expect these variables to be related. →

← *I've labeled my hy- potheses so that they are obvious to the reader.*

H1: Motives, attitudes, norms, behavioral control and affect will
predict a)political news use and b) political engagement.

Also, as Herr (1995) pointed out, it is unclear how affect is related to other ← *I justify my re- search question by explaining why it is a question rather than a clear conclusion that can be reached based upon the literature.*
variables that predict political behavior. Therefore, further research is needed

My hypothesis incorporates specific variables that I have conceptualized in the literature review

STEP 6

on how people's emotions are related to these variables that predict political engagement.

My research question is also labeled.

RQ1: How is affect related to motives, attitudes, norms, and behavioral control?

Lastly, research suggests that engaging younger people via new media may increase their sense of normative pressure and efficacy and increase political engagement.

H2: Young people who are engaged in political discussion and activity via social networks have more positive affect, feel more normative pressure, and feel more efficacy to a) follow political news and b) be politically engaged.

Conclusion

I review the main points discussed in the paper.

This paper reviewed different types of media use motives and TPB variables that explain political news use and other types of political engagement. These theories were used to explain how to get more young people involved in politics, particularly through use of early socialization in classrooms, from peers and parents, and through new media. These types of political activities could improve attitudes, norms, and efficacy related to political participation, thereby increasing engagement among younger generations. Clearly affect is an important variable that could add to the discussion about motives, attitudes, norms, and behavioral control. There is a genuine need to better understand young people's feelings about politics so that researchers are able to address the many reasons why some people are not participating in politics. Better understanding these reasons and using this research to design targeted political messages may help reach and involve younger citizens.

I reiterate the important findings that answer my overarching research question about how to get people involved in politics.

I also reiterate the direction that future research needs to go to address the problem that is the focus of my paper.

Notice that my references start on a new page. They are labeled "References." And "references" is not bold, italics, or underlined.

References

Ex-ample Refer-ence for a chapter in an edited book.

Delli Carpini, M. X. (2004). Mediating democratic engagement: The impact of communications on citizens' involvement in civic life. In L. L. Kaid (Ed.) *Handbook of political communication research* (pp. 395–434). Mahwah, NJ: Lawrence Erlbaum.

Example reference for a journal article.

Durnan, A., & Trafimow, D. (2000). Cognitive organization of favorable and unfavorable beliefs about performing a behavior. *The Journal of Social Psychology, 140,* 179–187.

Greenberg, B. S. (1974). Gratifications of television viewing and their correlates for British children. In J. G. Blumler & E. Katz (Eds.), *The uses of mass communication: Current perspectives on gratifications research.* Beverly Hills: Sage.

Herr, P. M. (1995). Whither fact, artifact, and attitude: Reflections on the theory of reasoned action. *Journal of Consumer Psychology, 4,* 371–380.

Lavine, H., Thomsen, C. J., Zanna, M. P., & Borgida, E. (1998). On the primacy of affect in the determination of attitudes and behavior: The moderating role of affective- cognitive ambivalence. *Journal of Experimental Social Psychology, 34,* 398–421.

Lee, N.-J., Shah, D. V., & McLeod, J. M. (2013). Processes of political socialization: A communication mediation approach to youth civic engagement. *Communication Research, 40,* 669-697. doi: 10.1177/0093650212436712

Notani, A. S. (1998). Moderators of perceived behavioral control's predictiveness in the theory of planned behavior: A meta-analysis. Journal of Consumer Psychology, 7, 247–271. doi: 10.1207/s15327663jcp0703_02

Palmgreen, P. (1984). Uses and gratifications: A theoretical perspective. *Communication Yearbook.* Retrieved from http://books.google.com/books?id=Hf2lYzR_i84 C&pg=PT76&dq=palmgreen+communication+yearbook&hl=en&sa=X&ei=Ij NoUvOkFqiQyAHpmIDQCw&ved=0CE0Q6AEwAQ#v=onepage&q=palmgr een%20communication%20yearbook&f=false

Perse, E. M. (1992). Predicting attention to local television news. *Communication Reports, 5,* 40–49.

Example reference for a website

Pew Research. (2012). Cable leads the pack as campaign news source: Twitter, Facebook play very modest roles. *Center for the People & the Press.* Retrieved from http://www.people-press.org/2012/02/07/section-1-campaign-interest-and-news- sources/

Rayburn, J. D., II, & Palmgreen, P. (1984). Merging uses and gratifications and expectancy-value theory. *Communication Research, 11,* 537–562.

POLITICAL PARTICIPATION AMONG YOUNG ADULTS   9

Rivis, A., Sheeran, P., & Armitage, C. J. (2009). Expanding the affective and normative
  components of the theory of planned behavior: A meta-analysis of anticipated affect
  and moral norms. *Journal of Applied Social Psychology, 39*, 2985–3019. doi: 10.1111/
  j.1559-1816.2009.00558.x
Rubin, A. M. (1984). Ritualized and instrumental television viewing. *Journal of
  Communication, 34*, 67–77.
Smith, A. (2013). Civic engagement in the Digital Age. *Pew Internet & American
  Life Project.* Retrieved from http://www.pewinternet.org/Reports/2013/Civic-
  Engagement/Summary-of-Findings.aspx
Taylor, P., & Lopez, M. H. (2013). Six take-aways from the Census Bureau's vot-
  ing report. *Pew Research Center.* Retrieved from http://www.pewresearch.org/
  fact tank/2013/05/08/six-take-aways-from-the-census-bureaus-voting-report/

STEP 7

The Seventh Step in Your Investigation: Edit Your Paper

Part of presenting the best possible case to your readers is to have a carefully edited paper. By this stage in the process, you are very close to and very involved in the project, and it is beneficial to have another, objective person look at your evidence, reasoning, and writing to offer feedback and advice on how to strengthen your case. Students can edit each others' work, go through drafts with their professors, visit their university's writing center, or even hire a professional editor to review their work. This unit goes over how to use different word processing software programs to work with editors or peers and provides a checklist to use to edit your own and others' work. But first, we will discuss the importance of peer review and working with a faculty mentor on your project.

You should also carefully edit your work. You should read through your paper several times to be sure it is clear, concise, conforms to APA style, and free of grammatical errors. Do not rely solely on spell check (for example, "spell cheek" isn't always underlined in red in word processing software!). And the following sentence is awful, but isn't underlined in green: "Common mistakes are plentiful, among my students, though I warn them!"

THIS CHAPTER COVERS:

A. Academe and Peer Review
B. Faculty Mentors
C. Tracking Reviews
    1. Using Track Changes and the Reviewing Pane in Microsoft Word®
    2. Editing in Adobe® pdf Documents
D. The "Three Read Rule"
    1. Read for APA Style
    2. Read for Formatting and Organization
    3. Read for Grammar, Punctuation, Voice, and Syntax

A. Academe and Peer Review

The cornerstone of academic research is the peer review process. **Peer reviewing** is when two or more people, with a background in an area of study relevant to the paper, provide feedback. Academic journal articles are peer reviewed by subject experts and by editors. Increasingly we use peer reviewing in our classrooms as well, for many of the same reasons we use peer review for academic publications. Though this process can be intimidating, and sometimes downright upsetting when the feedback is negative, it is done to ensure the quality of content. Research has suggested that peer review feedback is instructional to both the reviewer and the person whose work is being reviewed.

Peer reviewing is typically "blind," which means that the reviewers do not know whose work they are reviewing and the writers do not know who their reviewers are. Blind peer review, though it sometimes leads to harsh criticism of others' work, also ensures the anonymity of both the reviewer and the reviewee. This anonymity assures the reviewee that, even if the feedback is negative, his or her professional reputation will not be injured. For the reviewer, anonymity reduces the potential for biased reviews based on their personal relationships to, or history with, the writer, and also makes them more comfortable being frank and honest in their feedback.

Regardless of whether the review is blind or not, there are benefits to both the writer and the reviewer when we use peer review. For example, Cho and Cho (2011) studied the use of peer review in undergraduate writing and found that providing comments on the strengths and weaknesses of other students' work actually helped the students who were reviewing. In essence, by thinking critically about the quality of others' work, you yourself should become a better writer and researcher. So, by peer reviewing, you are not only helping improve the work of your peers, you are also learning ways that you can improve your own work. In addition, serving as a reviewer may help you learn about concepts and approaches to research that are less familiar to you, and may even give you ideas about topics that would be interesting to pursue in your own research.

Though there are many benefits to having your work reviewed and being a reviewer yourself, there are some guidelines to follow when reviewing that can help you and your peer get the most out of the process. Lee and Greenly (2009) pointed out that "reviews are only truly helpful if they are objective, constructive, [and] carried out in a neutral and unbiased way" that is beneficial to the author (p. 8). They offer some guidelines for peer review of academic work that apply very well to undergraduate peer review as well:

- You can express an opinion, but also be specific. Offer specific strengths and specific content that can be improved.
- Balance being supportive of your peers with being honest about their work.
- Reviewing does not necessarily mean that you "grade" their work.

The more specific you are while reviewing, the clearer it will be to your peers what they could do to improve their papers. So rather than vague comments such as, "the wording was unclear," give specific examples of places in the paper that were not clearly written. Offering these types of specific places that need improvement is important, but we also must balance that with a need to support each other through the process of writing. Pointing out strengths in the paper and avoiding criticisms that attack rather than instruct are two ways we can lessen the potential for hurt feelings.

B. Faculty Mentors

In addition to having and being a peer reviewer, junior scholars also benefit tremendously from having a faculty mentor to work with throughout the writing process, particularly when it is time to review the first draft of your paper. Like peer reviewing, mentoring is good for both you as a student and for the faculty member who mentors you. A mentor is someone who "provides the protégé with knowledge, advice, challenge, counsel, and support in the protégé's pursuit of becoming a full member of a particular profession" (Johnson, 2002, p. 88).

Part of having a faculty mentor is finding someone who is a good "fit" with your personality and your research interests. Mentors are often selective about their protégés, and so it is best to select a faculty mentor with whom you share a lot of commonalities and feel comfortable working. Here are some characteristics of a good mentor to help inform your choice (Johnson, 2002):

- They have clear expectations and are upfront about what they will do and what they expect from you as a student.
- They are patient and reassuring.
- They serve as models that you can follow in your own professional life.
- They are sensitive to gender and cultural differences.
- They have high expectations for you and for themselves, but accept and support you through challenges and failures.
- They politely step down as a mentor when they recognize that the relationship is not working.
- They do not exploit you, and remain objective and professional.

Having a relationship with a faculty mentor can help you cope with the stress of completing required research and writing assignments. These types of relationships are also valuable long-term professional relationships to have, as your mentor can help you hone your research and writing skills, offer you academic and professional advice, and serve as a reference for you when you are applying for jobs or graduate programs.

C. Tracking Reviews

Regardless of who is editing your work—whether it is a peer in your class, a faculty mentor, your class professor, or a writing tutor—it is helpful to know how to use and handle edits in different types of word processing software. We will focus here on Microsoft Word® and Adobe® pdf documents, though there are free software options, such as creating and sharing documents in Google Drive or Open Office.

There are essentially two options when reviewing another person's work: you can use track changes to make the changes yourself in Word® or you can use the comments function to point out things that need work or to make comments

STEP 7

on content. Typically, if you are conducting a peer *review*, using the comment function in either a .docx or .pdf format is ideal, because it gives the author the opportunity to see their mistake and correct it as they see fit.

That being said, if you are asked to *edit* another person's work, then using track changes in Word® (or using the mark-up options in Adobe®) may be appropriate. The writer will still have the option to accept or reject the changes that are made in the Word® document, and as long as you are sure that track changes is turned on, they will see every change you made in the document.

1. Using Track Changes and The Reviewing Pane in Microsoft Word®

Track changes is an option in Microsoft Word® that is available via the "Review" tab. Before beginning an edit of another person's work, turn track changes on. Any changes you make in the document will be highlighted. In addition to tracking changes, you can highlight text that you want to comment on, then select the "New" button under "Comments" to insert a comment. This can be helpful when you want to ask a question or make a general comment about content in the paper but you cannot, or do not want to, make the changes yourself while editing.

When you get a document back that has edits in track changes, all of the changes should be highlighted. You can right click on any of the changes and choose to accept or reject those modifications to your paper.

Example Comments and Edits in Word's® Reviewing Pane

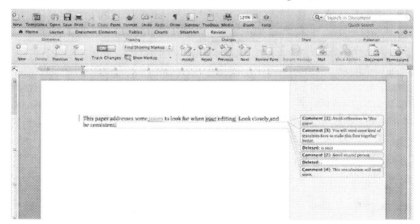

In this example of a reviewed and edited excerpt in Word®, I have made comments on the text and changed the text that needs to be corrected. The comments are numbered in the order that they appear in the text. The changes are made directly to the text, are called out in comment boxes in the side margin, and highlighted and underlined in the text itself. We can right click on any of the comments in the right margin to see the text that is being referred to, to delete a comment, or to accept/reject the changes that were made.

Guide to Select Features in Word's® Reviewing Pane

Editing and reviewing. Begin by turning tracking on. When you need to make a comment on the content being reviewed, highlight the text you want to comment upon and click the new comment button. You can type your comment directly into the comment box. You can modify the text itself as necessary, and any change you make will be noted in the comments.

Making corrections based on edits and reviews. When you receive a document back with changes and comments, the easiest way to handle it is to read through the entire document once. Look at each recommended change, and if you disagree with a particular change, reject it. Also while going through the paper, read the comments and consider the recommendations. Once you have thoroughly reviewed the entire document so that all of the comments were read and considered, modifications were made, and all of the changes you disagree with were rejected, you can simply delete all of the comments and accept all of the changes in the document. Delete all comments by clicking the gray arrow next to the delete comments icon in the toolbar. Select "Delete all comments in document" from the drop-down menu.

Here is a helpful resource for using the Reviewing Toolbar:
http://continuinged.uml.edu/online/tutorial/word_trackingxp/

Reviewing toolbar

STEP 7

Helpful Tip

Save each draft of your paper in a separate document and title documents according to date. For example, "Lit Review" becomes "Lit Review Oct 1," then "Lit Review Oct 15," etc. If you have a peer reviewer or mentor critiquing your work, you can also keep track of their contribution by noting in the title of the document whose edits you are incorporating (e.g., "Lit Review Prof C Comments Oct 19"). If you ever need a reminder about what has changed from one draft to another, use Word's "Merge Documents" feature, available in the "Tools" menu in Word. This will highlight the modified content.

© iQoncept, 2014. Shutterstock, Inc.

2. Editing in Adobe® pdf Documents

When people are using different types of word processing software that are not compatible, sometimes it is easier to save and share documents as pdfs and review and edit documents using that free software. The free version of Adobe® reader allows you to make annotations and markups on text, but not necessarily change the text in the same way that you can with Word's® track changes. This closely resembles older methods of grading with a red pen, and can be useful when sharing recommendations for improvements to a paper rather than personally editing a paper.

There are two features in Adobe's® reader that are useful when reviewing a paper: Annotations and markups. Annotations are changes that you recommend that are highlighted in the text and explained in the comments. Markups are actual markings that you make on the document. Both annotations and markups are listed in the "Comments List" on the right side of the pdf. Much like the features in Word®, you can click on each comment and it will highlight the associated text that is being marked up or annotated.

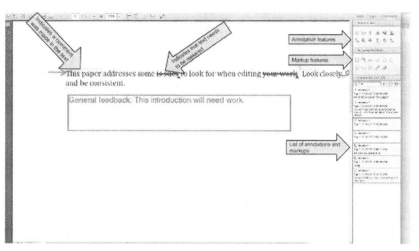

Example Annotations and Markups in a pdf Document

In this example pdf, I have added comments on the text using the "Comment" function. I have also indicated text that needs to be deleted and replaced using the "Replace text" function. I use the "Draw" function to indicate that the period needs to be removed, and the "Insert arrow" function to note that the paragraph needs to be indented. Lastly, I provided feedback directly on the document by inserting a textbox and writing my comments there. All of these changes and comments are listed in the sidebar, "Comments List."

Guide to Select Features in Adobe® pdf Documents

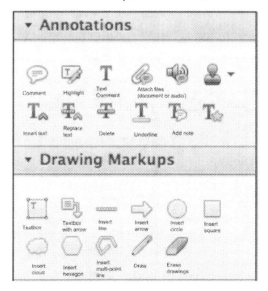

D. The "Three Read Rule"

Editing your own work involves striking a balance between disciplined self-reflection and awareness and not over-thinking or over-analyzing your own work. One tool that works well for us is the "three read rule." In this approach, we read through our own work three times, directing our attention to focus on different aspects of the paper each time.

Helpful Tip

Read once for references and citations.

Read a second time for formatting and organization.

Read a third time for writing and content.

© doomu, 2014. Shutterstock, Inc.

1. Read for APA Style

Citations. First, read through your paper, looking at the in-text citations and references. The in-text citations should follow these guidelines:

- Cite authors the first time you refer to one of their ideas.
- Only re-cite the same author if you have started a new paragraph and are still using their ideas *or* if you are moving back-and-forth between authors. It should always be clear to your reader which ideas are attributed to which authors.
- Never use authors' first names as part of in-text citations.
- Give the year of publication with the author(s) name.
- Follow the et al. rule.
- Every quote is marked with quotation marks and a page/paragraph number is given.
- Quotes are used sparingly, if at all.
- Any quote that is three or more lines long is a block quote, begins on a new line, and every line of the quote is indented 5 spaces.
- Check your in-text citations against your references.

> ### Final Warning: Check for Plagiarism
>
> Seasoned editors and professors are pretty good at spotting plagiarism in others' work. Here are some things we look for:
>
> - Phrases and sentences containing complex jargon
> - Phrases or statements we recognize from the literature
> - Changes in the tone, voice, or writing style in the paper

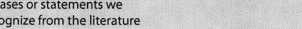

© Thomas Bethge, 2014. Shutterstock, Inc.

Plagiarism. We discussed plagiarism and the importance of paraphrasing when we went over tips for reading and taking notes on papers. When we edit our work, we should be alert to any unintentional plagiarism that may appear in our paper. Plagiarism is a big deal, and it's important that you and anyone you have editing your paper look closely at the use of source content and be sure that quotes are appropriately marked. You may have heard of the scandals that can erupt when work is plagiarized, such as Jayson Blair's resignation from *The New York Times*, and Fareed Zakaria's suspension from CNN for plagiarizing others' reporting. The stakes are very high and the consequences can be severe when we get caught plagiarizing, even if it is unintentional.

References. While you are checking your in-text citations against your references and ensuring the originality of your work, also check that your references conform to APA rules and match your citations. The reference list should follow these guidelines:

- Begin on a new page
- Labeled "References"
- First line is left justified; subsequent lines are indented for each reference
- The capitalization rules for chapter, website, and article titles are followed
- The capitalization and italicizing rules for book, journal, and website sources are followed
- The volume number, page numbers, web addresses, and doi numbers are given when required
- The content of every reference is accurate
- Everything in the list is double-spaced, and only double-spaced
- Check the reference list against the in-text citations

Checking citations and references: Use the "Find" function. The easiest way to check your references against your citations and your citations against your references is using the "find" function in Word® or Adobe®. As you read through your paper, type the name of each author in the "find" box (available under "Edit" in both the Word® and Adobe® toolbars). You can list matches in the sidebar in Word® (as shown below), and check to make sure that:

- The spelling of authors' names, years, etc. matches in both the in-text citations and references
- Everything that is cited in your paper appears in your reference list
- You follow the et al. rule for citations

Similarly, when you get to the reference list, search each author in your reference list using the "find" feature to be sure that everything in your reference list is cited somewhere in your paper. This is also a good time to double-check your APA style:

- References are in alphabetical order by first author's last name
- Reference formatting is correct:
  - First line of each reference is left justified
  - Subsequent lines in a given reference are indented
  - Rules for capitalization, italicizing, etc. are followed
- Each reference is complete:
  - Authors' names are correct; initials are given
  - Title of the chapter, article, or website is complete
  - Title of the book, journal, newspaper, or outlet is given
  - Volume numbers, page numbers, doi, and/or website is given where required

Example of Find Function in Word ©

2. Read for Formatting and Organization

When reading through your paper a second time, check to make sure that your main points are clear, they fit together, and that the paper is formatted correctly.

Beginning on the title page, compare your title page to the one in the example literature review in this book. Putting them next to each other, they should *look* the same. This is also true of your abstract page: it should look like the example abstract page in this book, with a label, about 100-word summary, and a labeled list of keywords.

In terms of looking at the organization and formatting in the paper, consider writing a reverse outline, or trying to create an outline of the paper based on what you are reading. Use headers to list the main points that you read, and fill in relevant sub-points under each main point as you read. Now, looking at your reverse outline, is the organization clear? Is it balanced? Do *all* of the main points lead up to the hypotheses, research questions, and/or conclusions you give at the end of the paper? This type of edit will help you reflect on the structure and coherence of your paper.

3. Read for Grammar, Punctuation, Voice, and Syntax

The last read through the paper is the closest and most careful. Here, we are looking for grammatical, punctuation, and syntax problems. Here are a few quick tips to help you identify common writing issues:

STEP 7

- **Use active voice.** If you can insert "by zombies" after the verb and still have a correct sentence, it is passive voice (The Writing Center, 2012). For example:
  ○ "Research conducted [by zombies] was conclusive" is passive voice.
  ○ "[Zombies] conducted conclusive research" is active voice.
- **Double-check punctuation.** A comma calls for a brief pause, semi-colons call for a medium-length pause, and a period means you must come to a complete stop when reading aloud (The Oatmeal 2013). When in doubt, read the sentence out loud to yourself: Does it *sound* like it needs a full stop, moderate-length pause, or only a brief pause?

Helpful Tip

Read your paper out loud to yourself. Even consider recording yourself and listening to the recording. Sometimes it's easier to *hear* when you're being wordy, unclear, or when there are issues with voice and syntax.

iQoncept, 2014. Shutterstock, Inc.

- **Check your apostrophes.** Apostrophes replace words or show possession for nouns and indefinite pronouns. They are also used in contractions; however, contractions should be avoided in formal writing. Apostrophes are never used with possessive pronouns, such as hers, his, ours, yours, its, etc.
- **Use semicolons sparingly.** Think of a semicolon as a "super-comma" that separates items in complex lists and can link together two closely related, but other-wise complete, sentences.

Check out this and other funny but useful advice from The Oatmeal.

- **Avoid bias and labeling.** The person always comes before the label. For example, "people who are disabled" is appropriate; "disabled people" is inappropriate.
- **Avoid ending sentences with prepositions**. We should not end sentences with words that explain how things are related: with, on, by, near, etc.
- **Always be clear who is doing the action**. Have a clear subject, or be clear *who* did *what*, in sentences. This avoids dangling modifiers.

- **Avoid run-on sentences**. If a sentence is over three lines long, it is likely a run-on sentence. Look for commas that signal interjections that could be removed, or conjunctions (such as and, or, but) that signal that two complete sentences may be unnecessarily linked together.
- **You, your, our, and we should not appear in your paper**.

REFERENCES

Cho, Y., & Cho, K. (2011). Peer reviewers learn from giving comments. *Instructional Science, 39*, 629–643.

Johnson, W. B. (2002). The intentional mentor: Strategies and guidelines for the practice of mentoring. *Professional Psychology: Research and Practice, 33*, 88–96.

Lee, N., & Greenly, G. (2009). Being a successful and valuable reviewer. *European Journal of Marketing, 43*, 5–10.

The Oatmeal. (2013). How to use a semicolon. Retrieved from http://theoatmeal.com/comics/semicolon

The Writing Center at American University. (2012). Identify passive voice (with zombies!). Retrieved from http://auwritingcenter.blogspot.com/2012/10/identify-passive-voice-with-zombies.html

ACTIVITIES

1. Editing Checklist
Use this Editing Checklist to complete three careful edits of your paper.

First Reading
Citations
- ____ Use only authors' last names, never first names
- ____ The spelling and order of authors' names is correct
- ____ Use et al. for three or more authors after citing them all the first time
- ____ Check the in-text citations against the reference list
- ____ Check the reference list against the in-text citations
- ____ Avoid quoting
- ____ Use quotation marks and give the page/paragraph number for all direct quotes

References
- ____ "References" is centered on the top of the reference page
- ____ The references start on a new page
- ____ References are all in alphabetical order by first author's last name
- ____ The first line of every reference is left justified

____ There is a hanging indent for the second line of each reference, and every line thereafter

____ The references follow the capitalization rules of APA for the article (or chapter) titles

____ The references follow the capitalization rules of APA for the source (book, website, or journal) titles

____ The volume number and page numbers are given when required (book chapters, articles, etc.)

____ The references follow the italicizing rules of APA

____ *Nothing* in the reference list, or paper, is underlined

____ The reference list is double-spaced, with no extra spaces between references

Second Reading

Format

____ Paragraphs are never more than one page, and never less than 2 sentences

____ The paper is typed in Times New Roman 12 pt or Arial 10 pt font

____ There is a cover page with the paper title, name, and the date in the center

____ There are page numbers in the upper right hand corner of every page, including the title page and reference page(s)

____ Paper has 1" margins

____ *Everything* in the paper is double-spaced; other than that there are *no* extra spaces

____ The paper is organized as follows: Title page, Abstract, Literature Review, References

Introduction

____ Clear attention getter

____ Clear thesis/purpose statement

____ Clear statement of importance/relevance

____ Clear preview of main points

Body of the Paper

____ Theories and variables are clearly defined and explained

____ Each main point clearly relates to the thesis/purpose

____ Main points are interrelated

____ Main points are well organized in a clear organizational pattern

____ Transitions are used throughout the paper

____ Articles are synthesized

____ There are clear, justified conclusions (hypotheses/research questions/ directions for future research)

Conclusion

____ There is a review of main ideas

____ There is a review of key findings/conclusions

____ The end makes an important point

Third Reading

Writing Style

____ Sentences are economical (not wordy)

____ Sentence structure is simple

____ Discussion of variables is clear, consistent, and correct

____ Word choice is correct throughout

____ Avoided labeling groups of people

____ Only used abbreviations after explaining them

____ Minimal use of first person (i.e., I, me, my, we)

____ Avoid second person (you, your)

Grammar and Punctuation

____ Subject and verb agreement (singular subjects get singular verbs)

____ Lists are in parallel form (all in the same tense)

____ Only capitalized proper nouns and words that began a sentence

____ Followed the rules for use of:

   ____ commas

   ____ quotation marks

   ____ semicolons

   ____ colons

2. Record, Replay, and Revise

Use a webcam to record yourself reading your paper out loud. Listen to the recording while you have your paper open on your computer. When you hear something that sounds long-winded, complicated, unclear, or awkward, pause the recording and go to that point in your paper and make corrections.

Re-record and listen to yourself reading the edited version of the paper to be sure that your paper is clear, concise, and correct.

STEP 8

The Eighth Step in Your Investigation: Present Your Findings

The culmination of an investigation is the presentation of the findings to share the evidence and offer a clear argument for your conclusions to others. There are several instances when you may be asked to present your research findings to others. While the basics of public speaking apply to each situation, there are particular guidelines to keep in mind in each context. For each context below, we will cover the purpose of the speech, how to effectively organize the speech, how to deliver the speech effectively, and how (and when) to incorporate visual aids.

THIS CHAPTER COVERS:

A. Poster Presentations
    1. Purpose
    2. Organization
    3. Delivery Style
    4. Visual Aids
B. Panel Presentations
    1. Purpose
    2. Organization
    3. Delivery Style
    4. Visual Aids
C. Individual Lectures/Presentations
    1. Purpose
    2. Organization
    3. Delivery Style
    4. Visual Aids
D. Online Presentations
    1. Purpose
    2. Organization
    3. Tips for Delivering a Speech with a Webcam
    4. Uploading Videos to YouTube
    5. Some Great Examples of Online Presentations

A. Poster Presentations

1. Purpose

Poster presentations are a great way to present research visually. They are also excellent ways to discuss your research with others in a more one-on-one manner. Posters are a very flexible method of presentation, yet there are some guidelines to follow in order to make your poster a success. For more details on how to design a professional poster, you can access the National Communication Association's *Creating a Scholar to Scholar Poster:*

A Guide for Beginners at http://www.natcom.org/uploaded Files/PDF-CRL-%20Creating_a_Successful_S2S_Poster%20_revised .pdf

NCA Poster Guidelines

2. Organization

Posters can range in size from smaller tri-fold designs to larger, professional style posters. Regardless of the size of poster you plan to present, you should carefully plan your presentation to engage your audience. Essentially, you should examine the content you wish to display, how you wish to organize the content, and the design elements of the poster.

- **Content.** Think of your poster as an abstract for your paper. As with an abstract, you want to highlight all the important information that would draw an audience to your work. Information that might be included is the rationale for your study, the theoretical perspectives used, the methodology applied, the key findings, and discussion points. There is a great degree of flexibility with a poster presentation—choose the most engaging and important content to display. The main focus of the poster should be on your findings, since this is typically what will interest people the most.

   In some instances, you might not be standing by your poster at all times. You may be asked to put your poster up for an entire conference session. If you are not sure if this is a possibility, you want to make sure that your poster includes enough content that will allow a person to understand your project without clarification from you.

Caution

Do not simply copy and paste your entire paper onto a poster. The goal is to showcase your project and engage the audience, not to have them read the paper word-for-word. When appropriate, you can provide interested parties with a copy of your work after your poster presentation.

© Thomas Pajot, 2014. Shutterstock, Inc.

- **Organization.** The organization of your poster is very important. Any person walking past your work should easily be able to identify the title of the poster, as well as what your project entails. You can't include everything from your paper in the poster—so think of how you could use bullet points and key factors that would be most engaging. Key portions of your poster should stand out to passersby. Also, remember that people read left to right or top to bottom, so you want to make sure your content flows accordingly.
- **Design.** The choices you make regarding design can make or break a poster. Decisions regarding font size, color, and graphics should be made with care.
  - **Font.** When you choose a font size, you want to make sure that your poster is easily readable from a few feet away. Most people browse through a poster session and will only come closer if they feel the topic is interesting to them. Therefore, the title of your poster should really be the focal point. The major sections should also stand out so that readers can go directly to what interests them the most.
  - **Color.** Color should be used throughout to engage the audience. Color can be used as a background or to highlight specific words or topics within the poster. However, the use of white space should not be underestimated. You don't want your poster to appear crammed with information. Be sure to contrast the font color with the background—use light fonts with dark backgrounds, and vice versa.
  - **Graphics.** Graphics, including charts and graphs, are highly recommended in a poster format. The old adage that "a picture is worth a thousand words" is certainly true when it comes to poster presentations. Take advantage of the visual format and include colorful charts or pictures to display your research topic.

Here is a good example of the use of graphics to draw attention to the parts of a poster: http://jasonthamdotcom.files. wordpress.com/2013/11/nca-scholar-to-scholar.jpg

Poster graphics

3. Delivery Style

Poster sessions can be a low-pressure form of presentation for those who like one-on-one communication. During a poster session, attendees will usually come up to engage you in your work. This allows for more in-depth discussion and connection with those who have similar interests. This also means that you need to be well-informed and well-prepared to discuss your project in detail when asked.

Poster sessions usually lend themselves to a more conversational delivery style. This does not mean, however, that you can be unprofessional. Like all the forms of presentation discussed in this chapter, you should be aware of your physical and vocal delivery. Use effective speaking and listening skills to be able to engage in effective communication with your audience.

Tip

Public speaking skills are necessary for a successful presentation. For a thorough overview of speaking skills, reference a public speaking textbook or visit this open source website: http://www.publicspeakingproject.org/.

© Modella, 2014, Shutterstock, Inc.

4. Visual Aids

Poster design can vary depending on the purpose of the presentation. Typically at professional conferences, a more formal poster may be required. For a class presentation or colloquium, tri-fold or poster boards might be appropriate. You want to be sure of size requirements and any equipment that might be needed before designing your poster. You wouldn't want to design a tri-fold and find out that the conference doesn't support tables for their posters. Regardless of the format, you want to adhere to the previously discussed recommendations regarding font, color, and graphics.

Poster templates can be incredibly helpful when designing a poster. There are excellent poster templates available online or through your word processing/ presentation software. Microsoft's PowerPoint® offers many options for poster templates. If you do not have Microsoft Office® (or you prefer other options) many good templates can be found for free or for a small cost online. However, remember that you are smarter than the computer. Many templates are not effective and may not fit your needs. Feel free to modify a template to fit your project.

Below is an example of a large format poster presented at the National Communication Association conference. Notice the title bar that includes the paper title, the authors, and graphics of the authors' institutions. Also note the use of color to highlight key sections and words, as well as the use of models to demonstrate the purpose of the study as well as the important findings.

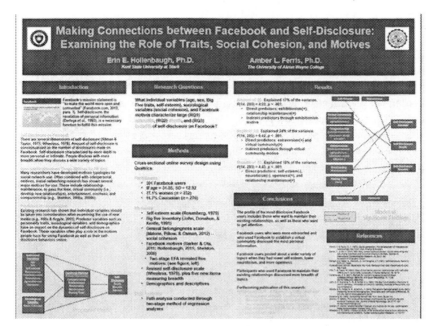

B. Panel Presentations

1. Purpose

Panel presentations are useful in any situation where a group of presenters wishes to cover various angles of a broader topic. A panel presentation involves a small number of presenters, typically 5 or 6, who discuss their work one by one. Oftentimes panel presentations include a question and answer session at the end where audience members can gather further information if needed. Panel presentations tend to be more formal than poster presentations, and are usually much more structured. We'll discuss how to present effectively within this context next.

2. Organization

One of the most common panel presentations is the conference presentation. Here, scholars present original work to an audience. All of the papers on a panel are typically organized around a common theme. For example, a conference panel might be discussing papers on reality television, or the latest presidential election, and each paper on that panel will be a study that fits that broad theme. If you decide to present your paper at a conference—and we hope you do—make a note of the theme for the panel as you decide how you are going to organize and present your paper.

A conference presentation of original research is typically about 12 to 15 minutes long, and there is usually time allotted after the presentation for questions. As with the poster sessions, the National Communication Association offers some great advice for presenting papers at a conference: http://www.natcom.org/Tertiary.aspx?id=1763. While conference presentations are the most common panel presentations in an academic setting, you might also be asked to convey research in a panel format in your classes as well as in professional settings. Regardless of the format, the guidelines presented below will help you be a success.

Conference papers

Essentially, a panel presentation combines the organization of a research paper with the skills of public speaking. Your goal is to convey the information of your paper in a clear, concise, and interesting manner. To this end, you should consider the following when constructing your presentation:

- **The panel guidelines.** Consider how many presenters are on the panel and how much time you will be allotted to speak. Do not be inconsiderate of others—if there is a time constraint, you should adhere to it. Also remember the panel title. You should stick to the topic of the panel and to your paper and refrain from diverging off-topic.
- **The audience.** The audience should always be considered when organizing a panel presentation. Are they experts in this area, or are they fairly inexperienced? The language you choose and the level of detail you go into are highly dependent on the audience. For example, certain statistical information or theoretical perspectives may be common knowledge to a room full of academics, but may need to be clarified to a room full of practitioners. You cannot be effective if your audience does not connect with your topic. Remember—the audience members are there because they are interested in hearing what you have to say. Your job is to convey that information in the most effective manner possible.
- **Be organized.** Constructing a presentation requires good organizational skills. In any presentation, what you are essentially doing is making an argument. You have a goal or a purpose, and you organize your presentation around that goal to argue effectively. Organizational patterns are the method to achieving a clear argument. By utilizing both public speaking and research writing patterns, you can organize a clear and interesting panel presentation.
    - ○ **Introduction.** This is where you make your argument clear. The introduction should include the rationale for your study, why you chose to study it, a thesis statement that outlines your argument, and a preview of your main points. The audience should know exactly what you plan to discuss after hearing your introduction. Remember to engage your audience in the introduction—grab their interest right in the beginning!

○ **Main points.** Typically, your main points will come from the construction of your paper. For example, your main points might be the theoretical perspective used in the paper, a brief overview of important studies supporting your topic, the methodology used, and your results. Consider the most interesting aspects of your paper. You can't possibly cover everything you wrote—think of what the audience would need to know to understand your argument.

Remember

Don't forget the power of transitions between key parts of your speech: the introduction, each main point, and the conclusion! When your speech flows smoothly, your audience will be able to follow you.

© imagineerinx, 2014. Shutterstock, Inc.

○ **Conclusion.** Conclusions are a summation of your argument. Here you should discuss the implications of your results, discuss any important limitations, and/or give the audience some directions for future research. Leave the audience with a lasting impression of your work.

• **Enhance your credibility.** Including citation of your sources is a must; citations enhance both your credibility as a speaker and the credibility of your research. You should give credit to those ideas that support your own—remember that the audience does not have your paper in front of them. Your oral citation is the only means they have of knowing what ideas are yours and those that come from others. Whether your audience has expert knowledge in your topic or they are new to it, providing citations to support your claims is a must.

3. Delivery Style

A panel presentation is a public speech; therefore, the guidelines for giving a speech will be most useful to those planning to present on a panel. While this may be more intimidating for some, it is a great way to get your work out to the most people at one time. When presenting on a panel, you should use an extemporaneous delivery style. Extemporaneous delivery should be conversational and relatable. Being **conversational** means that you should use language that is appropriate to yourself and the audience, use variety in vocal quality (i.e., vary your pitch, volume, and pace), and use appropriate physical behaviors such as engaging in eye contact and gesturing.

One big mistake some presenters make during panel presentations is that they read their paper word-for-word. Reading your paper is inappropriate because you are not connecting with the audience. And, as you can probably guess, we don't write like we speak. Therefore, reading a paper word-for-word tends to be very boring for an audience. If you are tempted to read your paper, you should construct an outline using the guidelines for organization discussed previously. This outline should include keywords that will trigger your memory for each important section of your presentation. You should only include full sentences when it is very important that the information be read completely (i.e., citations, statistics, and direct quotations).

Public speaking anxiety. Panel presentations can often induce anxiety in some people. It is important to remember that the fear of public speaking is common and quite normal. However, if you feel that your anxiety may be problematic, you should seek help through your university or department. There are also many online resources available to help you. For example, the Toastmasters organization offers some general tips to relieve anxiety: http://www.toastmasters.org/tips.asp.

Toastmasters

The National Communication Association has many useful resources to help when developing your presentation. NCA has identified 8 competencies that should be met in order to deliver an effective speech. These competencies are outlined in the following rubric. You can use this rubric when practicing your speech. Additional information regarding these competencies can be found at http://www.natcom. org/uploadedFiles/Teaching_and_Learning/Assessment_Resources/ PDF-Competent_Speaker_Speech_Evaluation_Form_2ndEd.pdf

NCA competencies

IV. The NCA Competent Speaker Speech Evaluation Form

Course:_____ Semester:_____ Date:_____ Project:_____
Speaker(s):_____

PRESENTATIONAL COMPETENCIES	RATINGS		
	Unsatisfactory	Satisfactory	Excellent
Competency One: CHOOSES AND NARROWS A TOPIC APPROPRIATELY FOR THE AUDIENCE & OCCASION			
Competency Two: COMMUNICATES THE THESIS/SPECIFIC PURPOSE IN A MANNER APPROPRIATE FOR THE AUDIENCE & OCCASION			
Competency Three: PROVIDES SUPPORTING MATERIAL (INCLUDING ELECTRONIC AND NON-ELECTRONIC PRESENTATIONAL AIDS) APPROPRIATE FOR THE AUDIENCE & OCCASION			
Competency Four: USES AN ORGANIZATIONAL PATTERN APPROPRIATE TO THE TOPIC, AUDIENCE, OCCASION, & PURPOSE			
Competency Five: USES LANGUAGE APPROPRIATE TO THE AUDIENCE & OCCASION			
Competency Six: USES VOCAL VARIETY IN RATE, PITCH, & INTENSITY (VOLUME) TO HEIGHTEN & MAINTAIN INTEREST APPROPRIATE TO THE AUDIENCE & OCCASION			
Competency Seven: USES PRONUNCIATION, GRAMMAR, & ARTICULATION APPROPRIATE TO THE AUDIENCE & OCCASION			
Competency Eight: USES PHYSICAL BEHAVIORS THAT SUPPORT THE VERBAL MESSAGE			

4. Visual Aids

Visual aids are becoming more popular in panel presentations; however, a visual aid is not always needed in this format. If you decide that a visual aid would be helpful to your audience, here are some considerations to keep in mind.

- **Use presentation software.** Panel presentations can have very large audiences, so posters or objects are typically not effective. PowerPoint®, Prezi®, or other types of presentation slideware are preferred. If you decide to use presentation software, be sure to check the venue for technology availability.
- **Remember the purpose of a visual aid.** A visual aid should AID you, not replace you. Avoid full sentences on slides; your natural tendency is to read them (see delivery tips). Use slides to your advantage to help the audience follow along with your presentation and enhance interest in your topic.
- **Visual aids should be clean, professional, and simple.** Your audience shouldn't have to work to understand your slides. Here are some tips to keep in mind:
  - **Avoid excessive animation.** While you might think it adds interest to have bells and whistles zing or words in and out, it is very distracting to the audience. Use animation sparingly (if at all).
  - **Avoid distracting images or graphics.** If you include graphics or images, they should be relevant to the content. You might be tempted to put a cute kitten on a slide or a funny cartoon to get the audience to pay attention, but remember that you are giving a professional presentation. Any graphics or images should add appropriate interest.
  - **Avoid charts, graphs, or models that are really complex.** If a chart can't fit on a slide without reducing the font size, it probably isn't a good idea to include it. Remember, if the audience can't read the font, the aid is not working.
  - **Use appropriate fonts, colors, and backgrounds.** Regarding font, avoid script fonts or fonts that are not standard (such as the Chiller font for Halloween). Unique fonts may not translate on screen as well. Standard Arial, Times New Roman, or Bookman fonts are easier to read. As with poster recommendations regarding color, slides should use a light font with a dark background, or dark font on a light background and should incorporate white space for easy reading. Avoid busy backgrounds or templates. When it comes to slides, simple is always better. Let your research be the star, not an over-the-top presentation aid.

C. Individual Lectures/Presentations

1. Purpose

In a classroom setting, it is probably more common to give an individual presentation of your research findings than a panel presentation. Also, someday you might need to give a lecture on your research. While many of the tips related to panel presentations still hold true, there are some specific guidelines to presenting in this context.

2. Organization

One major difference between the panel presentation and an individual lecture is the time frame. Typically, individual lectures tend to be longer in length. Whereas panel presentations tend to be no longer than 15 minutes, individual presentations can last up to an hour. Because you have more time, the content of your presentation can be much more detailed.

The key to organizing an individual presentation is to remember the reason you are speaking. Are you summarizing a body of work, or discussing a specific study? Are you speaking to peers, experts, or the general public? As with panel presentations, you should analyze your audience to deliver the speech at the appropriate level.

In addition to the organizational tips given previously, here are a few specific guidelines for individual presentation organization:

- **Introducing yourself.** You may need to give a brief biography of who you are before diving into the subject matter. This is especially important if you were not introduced by a host. If you do need to discuss who you are, make sure you pick the information that is most relevant to the audience (for example, what institution or organization you belong to, degrees earned, areas of study, etc.).
- **Main points.** Choose main points wisely. You have a forum to be more detailed, but don't bore your audience with minor details. If you are presenting research, focus on the results and the implications of these results. More details regarding theory and/or methodology may be appropriate, but remember that the audience can always request your paper if they want more information.
- **Timing.** Keep in mind the time you were allotted and do your best to meet that time requirement. Find out if there is an opportunity for questions, and be sure to clarify if that is part of your total time frame. Practice—the last thing you want to do is go significantly over or under your allowed time.

3. Delivery Style

As with panel presentations, you want to use extemporaneous delivery. You want to seem as if you are speaking *with* the audience, *not at them*. This can be hard to convey in a lecture, but by engaging in eye contact, using proper gestures, and engaging with the audience whenever appropriate, you can enhance your delivery style. Avoid reading from a manuscript; using a keyword outline is more desirable.

The contextual factors of your speech may be very important when giving an individual lecture or presentation. These factors include things like the environment you are speaking in, whether there is a microphone, a podium, and the availability of computer technology. Here are some tips to deal with these common contextual variables.

- **Environmental factors**. The size and layout of the room you will speak in can have a large impact on your delivery style. If the room is very large, you may want to request a microphone to be able to project clearly to everyone in the room. Even in a smaller room, if you happen to be soft-spoken, a microphone might be a good idea. If you are in a lecture hall with a stage, be sure to note the dimensions of it (the last thing you want to do is fall off the stage while speaking!). If everyone is on the same level, consider moving around to be able to engage everyone in the audience.
- **Microphones.** Using a microphone can be challenging, but very beneficial. Remember to place the microphone in a position that allows you to project sound appropriately. Test it before you speak in order to find the perfect position. Many people make the mistake of talking too closely into a microphone, and it can distort your voice or make it inaudible. If you are clipping your microphone onto a shirt or suit, remember when it is on! You don't want to make any inappropriate comments or personal statements while you are still "live."
- **Podiums.** Podiums are highly beneficial when giving a lecture; they allow you to use your speaking notes effectively and many people feel more comfortable speaking when they have a podium. Remember to use the podium as a tool to help you—not a lifeline. Avoid gripping the podium or standing stiffly behind it the entire speech. If you have room, move around from time to time. This helps you engage with the audience and appear more conversational.
- **Computer technology.** In the next section we'll discuss visual aids, but one factor you must know before giving a lecture is the availability of technology. If you have specialized needs (Mac or PC, availability of PowerPoint®, etc.), you should check with your host prior to the speech. Never assume a university classroom or conference center has the ability to use slideware, specific computer programs, or even wireless internet. Requests can usually be made ahead of time to ensure you are able to use technology as you wish.

4. Visual Aids

Visual aids are extremely helpful in a lecture/individual presentation format. Because these speeches tend to be longer, a visual aid can help maintain audience interest. While the previously discussed information on visual aids holds true in this context, here are some unique opportunities for visual aids with the lecture format:

- **Think outside the box.** Slideware products like PowerPoint® and Prezi® are highly recommended. However, because lectures have the advantage of time, think of how you might incorporate interactivity or videos into your presentation. Be creative, but appropriate. You are still giving a professional presentation but, whenever possible, incorporate visuals to engage your audience.
- **Consider context.** As with your delivery considerations, think about the placement of the projection screen to the audience, the availability of technology, and the room size when designing visual aids. If the projection screen is on the same level as the audience, be wary of putting text too low; people in the back will most likely not be able to see it. Also consider the lighting of the room, especially when using color in your slides. If the room does not have dimmers above the projection screen or is very bright, consider using a white background with dark lettering. If the room is fairly dark, choose a darker background color and lighter fonts.
- **Dress.** Regardless of the presentation type, it's usually a good idea to dress business casual. This means no t-shirts and jeans. How you dress does communicate something about you, and you want to be sure to present your best self when discussing important topics like your research. When giving an individual lecture, a suit may be more appropriate. Even if not required in a classroom setting, a suit is never a bad choice. This is because a suit conveys professionalism.

Dress comfortably! Choose comfortable shoes; during many lectures, you will be standing while speaking, so you don't want to be in pain the whole time. Don't wear clothes that are too tight or too loose. If you choose a skirt or dress

Tip

Not sure what is appropriate business casual attire? Check out this helpful website from Virginia Tech on the subject. While these guidelines focus on job interviews, the principles relate directly to dressing for a professional presentation. http://www.career.vt.edu/JobSearchGuide/BusinessCasualAttire.html

© Fejas, 2014. Shutterstock, Inc.

option, be sure the length of the outfit is appropriate (typically, at least knee-length) and you are not showing too much skin. When in doubt about what to wear, don't hesitate to ask the host of the lecture. It is far better to ask beforehand so you can be prepared than to be underdressed.

D. Online Presentations

We no doubt live in a technologically connected society, so the likelihood you will someday give an online presentation is very high. Two common forms of online presentations are YouTube videos and webinars.

1. Purpose

If you want to reach a large audience with your research, you might want to consider uploading a presentation to YouTube. Recording your presentation and posting it on websites like YouTube can be great way to get your ideas to the masses. The advantage to using this format is that you can polish your presentation and edit it to convey your exact message. A disadvantage to consider is that once something is presented online it will last forever, so you want to take great care in how you construct this presentation.

Webinars can also reach a large audience, but they are often done in "real time." Audience members can tune in to watch you present at locations all over the world. The advantage to webinars is the live audience. The audience can often interact directly with the presenter and vice versa.

2. Organization

Webinars are organized in the same manner as an individual lecture. Because you have already been introduced to those skills, this section will focus on organizing YouTube presentations. There are a few options when it comes to organizing a YouTube presentation.

The first option is to record yourself in a realistic setting, such as a face-to-face lecture. The advantage of this style is that your delivery tends to be more natural. However, depending on the camera angle and sound quality, a realistic setting may not be the best choice. The online audience may not be able to see you or your visual aid, which will negatively impact your presentation. Also, you have less flexibility with editing because the video was shot live.

Another option is to record your presentation using video capture software such as Panopto® or Camtasia®. These programs allow you to record audio while simultaneously capturing images from your computer. These images may include slideware, videos, charts, spreadsheets, pictures—anything you do on your computer during the lecture will be recorded. Check with your university for video capturing software; you may have access to this type of technology. The advantage to using this type of presentation is that you can edit your presentation and record it as often as you want to get it perfect. You also have a great deal of flexibility when it comes to using visual aids. The main disadvantage to this type of presentation is that you may lose connection with your audience since you are not physically shown.

A last option is to merge the two styles: lecture to the camera and incorporate screenshots and/or visual aids. Essentially, you are speaking directly to your audience, but you can incorporate visual techniques if needed. This style will allow you to "connect" to your audience since they are able to see you. You can utilize a webcam or video production equipment. For a more professional presentation, you may want to consult a videographer or someone with advanced video skills to produce your video. This can be expensive, but your university may have a studio that can help you create and edit your work.

3. Tips for Delivering a Speech with a Webcam

Because webcams are probably the most common form of available technology to record an online presentation, we'll discuss some unique delivery aspects to keep in mind. While many of the tips you have already learned about delivery and research presentations still apply, there are special considerations while using a webcam.

- **Be aware of your surroundings.** Whether you are taping a video for You-Tube or presenting live via webcast, you want to make sure your audience can see you properly. In an article on CBS.com, Turmel (2010) suggests using a light source in front of you to avoid shadows and so that you come in clear on camera. Also, be sure to check your background. What will the audience see behind you? Art? A bookshelf? A poster of Justin Bieber? Avoid background clutter or images that are not relevant to your discussion. Choose a private area where people will not be walking behind you. Avoid any background noises that might be distracting, including TV or radio noise, and all other technology - including your phone.
- **Consider your physical and vocal delivery.** With regards to gesturing or movements, you want to be natural and not robotic. Be sure to move slowly—webcams can sometimes have a lag or have trouble tracking fast or erratic movements. This is especially true when recording live. Turmel (2010) states that many webcams do not have high resolution, which may cause the picture to blur or break up. Because of this fact, you want to maintain as much extemporaneous delivery as possible. This includes using vocal variety and volume appropriately. Be sure to test the sound quality of your video before recording. If necessary, use a microphone to enhance your volume. Lastly, be careful if you are reading from a script. It may be tempting to script your presentation—but just as it would be face-to-face, reading a manuscript can lead to a monotonous tone of voice

and less connection to the audience. Consider using keyword outlines for content rather than a word-for-word manuscript.

- **Dress appropriately.** Colors matter when it comes to using a webcam. Wear solid colored clothing rather than white or patterned/checkered clothes. All-white or patterned clothes can appear distorted on camera and will be an unnecessary distraction to viewers. Remember that you are presenting in a professional situation, so you should review the previous guidelines for appropriate dress.

- **Engage in eye contact.** Remember to look into the webcam and speak straight into the lens—not your picture. On programs like Skype you can often see yourself in the corner of your screen. Remember to avoid talking to your image and "engage" with your audience. Turmel suggests incorporating a visual aid to add focus to your material and away from you. Programs like Panopto® or Camtasia® will allow you to show slideware while you talk, which can be very helpful to the audience. However, you still may want to give a clear introduction and conclusion face-to-face in order for the audience to feel a connection to you as the speaker. If you are engaging in a question and answer session, be sure to turn the camera back to face-to-face mode.

- **Be prepared for problems.** This is especially important in a live webinar or webcast. Internet connections may lag and computers may have issues. While you hope these issues do not arise, you should be prepared in the event that they might. Certainly you will want to fully test your equipment prior to "going live," but the best-laid plans can still be thwarted by technology. Turmel (2010) has a great suggestion to keep an appropriate still picture on hand to display in the event that the live feed has issues.

While some presentations you might give will be live or in real-time, many of you may choose to tape and/or edit a presentation for upload to YouTube. The following discussion will outline how to do this, should you be interested in sharing your research with the internet world.

4. Uploading Videos to YouTube

YouTube is one of the world's largest video sharing websites. In March 2013, YouTube hit a milestone traffic marker, with 1 billion unique visitors accessing the website each month (Reuters, 2013). If you want to get your research out there to many people, YouTube might be your best bet. Of course, before jumping into the YouTube universe, you will want to read through their terms and conditions carefully. You can access this information at http://www.youtube.com/t/community_guidelines.

YouTube Community guidelines

To begin uploading videos, you will first need to create an account and your personal YouTube channel. This allows you to have a profile and for people to subscribe to your talks. You might find that you enjoy discussing your research in this format, and others may want to hear more of what you are presenting. Channels allow others to follow you. To get help on setting up an account on YouTube, visit this link: https://support.google.com/youtube/answer/161805?hl=en&ref_topic=1360734

Scan here to access YouTube's help page that details how to set up an account and your own YouTube channel.

You will need a valid email address to create a channel. Once you input your email address and create a password, you can create a basic profile. After you click continue, you will be taken to a screen that allows you to upload your videos: https://support.google.com/youtube/answer/57924?hl=en.

Scan here to access YouTube's help page on how to upload a video.

Once you are here, you are ready to begin uploading. You can choose any video you have saved or previously recorded or, as you can see on the right hand side, YouTube does offer video production and editing tools that may be helpful to you. Note that you can upload videos up to 15 minutes in length with a new account, or if you verify your account, you can post longer videos.

Privacy settings are important to consider when uploading videos to YouTube. The default setting is set to Public. This means that everyone on YouTube can access your video. Unlisted videos will not be searchable, and only those with whom you share the URL link to your video can access it. That being said, anyone who is given the URL will be able to see the video. If a friend that you have sent the link to posts the link on a social network, others will be able to click on it and view your material. If you choose the Private setting, only select users that you choose will be able to access your video. For further details regarding privacy, see YouTube's guidelines at https://support.google.com/youtube/answer/157177?hl=en.

YouTube privacy guidelines

After you have chosen your privacy settings, you are free to upload your video. Remember to upload your final, polished version that is ready for the public. Also, remember that *once you upload something to the internet, it lasts forever.* Even if you choose at some point to take your video down, it still exists in the cyberworld someplace. Consider this carefully before uploading anything to YouTube or any other website.

5. Some Great Examples of Online Presentations

TED is a nonprofit organization dedicated to recording interesting presentations on topics they view as "Ideas Worth Spreading" (Ted.com, n.d.). They post their free access

TedX web site

discussions online at www.ted.com or via YouTube. We've selected a few related to communication that you might find helpful should you be interested in recording a webinar or online presentation yourself.

Opening new organizational communication loops: Sarah Magill at TEDxCoMo. Available on YouTube at http://www. youtube.com/watch?v=LImUb_yf_ps

Connected, but alone? Sherry Turkle. Available at http://www. ted.com/playlists/26/our_digital_lives.html

TEDxBerkeley—Neha Sangwan—The Communication Cure. Available at http://www.youtube.com/watch?v=LOZ84ZfDqKM

DeDe Wohlfarth Channel: **gender communication 1** YouTube link: http://www.youtube.com/watch?v=Iz9NmfEAsso

kk Bay Channel: **CAT THEORY** YouTube link: http://www. youtube.com/watch?v=0VaKftk9p08

REFERENCES

Reuters. (2013, March). YouTube says has 1 billion monthly active users. Retrieved from http://www.reuters.com/article/2013/03/21/us-youtube-users-idUSBRE92K0 3O20130321

TED (n.d.) About TED. Retrieved from http://www.ted.com/pages/about

Turmel, W. (2010, July). 8 tips for presenting with a webcam. Retrieved from http://www. cbsnews.com/news/8-tips-for-presenting-with-a-web-cam/

ACTIVITIES

1. Test your poster evaluation skills by examining this conference poster:

http://colinpurrington.com/wp-content/uploads/2012/02/bad-scientific-poster-example.jpg

A) What aspects of the poster, if any, did you find effective?

B) What aspects of the poster were ineffective?

Conference poster

2. Here are YouTube videos for you to analyze. Consider applying the speaking rubric in this chapter as well as the knowledge you have learned about online presentations in your evaluation. These examples range from students' to college professors' presentations. None of them are perfect; but there are both good points to incorporate and some mistakes to avoid. Try not to focus on the content per se, but on their delivery and use of technology.

Mass Media Theories, commrap Channel: **Herman and Chomsky's Propaganda Model** YouTube link: http://www.youtube.com/watch?v=zGgkGmSmR8w&list=PL46448E85E02A0160

LEZakel Channel: **Johari Window in Interpersonal Communication** YouTube link: http://www.youtube.com/watch?v=-7FhcvoVK8s

YouTube Video: Ec ho Channel: **HLTH 452 Panel Presentation – 2013** YouTube link: http://www.youtube.com/watch?v=QjDX-IbVz7s

Ec ho Channel:
HLTH 452 Panel
Presentation

Conclusion

WHERE TO FROM HERE?

Your final paper and presentation should represent the culmination of valuable skills that you have developed:

- Comprehension of communication concepts and research methods
- Writing skills
- Researching skills
- Critical thinking abilities
- Speaking skills using presentation technologies

There are several directions to go from here. Often the literature review is the first step to a larger, original research project. You could conduct a small case study or a larger social scientific study by developing a method section and collecting data. If you have enjoyed the process of researching and writing, you may also consider making a career in the field doing things like blogging, professional writing, and editing. Even if your literature review is an end in and of itself, you can use it in your professional portfolio as evidence of your writing abilities and ability to find, interpret, integrate, and present complex information.

THIS CHAPTER COVERS:

A. Your Literature Review as a First Step Toward a Research Study
　　1. Using What You've Learned in Your Literature Review: The Case Study Approach
B. Professional Uses of Writing and Presenting Skills
　　1. Using Research Skills as a Blogger
　　2. Using Research Skills for Fact Checking and Copy Editing
C. Present Your Research in a Professional and/or Academic Portfolio
　　1. Social Networks
　　2. Portfolio-Building Websites
　　3. Websites
D. Concluding Thoughts

A. Your Literature Review as a First Step Toward a Research Study

Often, literature reviews are the first step toward designing and conducting a full research study. Though literature reviews may be an end in and of themselves, such as a retrospective or historical piece on a communication theory or a meta-analysis of an area of research, literature reviews are often the foundation on which academic studies are built.

The suggestions and guidelines offered here are intended to help you build a literature review that would support a larger study. Advanced study in research design, methods, and (if quantitative) statistics may be necessary before taking the next steps toward a full study. That being said, we have covered methods of historical research and qualitative coding in this book that would aid you in conducting a case study.

1. Using What You've Learned in Your Literature Review: The Case Study Approach

Case studies are when we apply academic concepts to explore critically a specific situation, event, or artifact. For example, we could use our literature review about political engagement among American youth to conduct a case study of a presidential election.

You can see some examples of case studies in our discipline by browsing through recent publications in *Case Studies in Strategic Communication:* http://cssc.uscannenberg.org. As they point out on their website, "Case studies illustrate the strategies, tactics, and execution of communication campaigns through in-depth coverage of a single situation." Put another way, case studies apply what we know about communication concepts to real life events to help us understand what happened and why. Case studies aren't limited to campaigns and media events either. Interpersonal case studies are also common.

Case studies are an excellent application of the research you have done for your literature review for a couple of reasons. First, you have developed clear conceptualizations of the variables related to your problem question. Having a clear, research-based knowledge of theories and concepts is the first step to applying those theories and concepts to understand real people and events. Second, you have seen how other researchers have operationalized those concepts. Given that you know how things are measured or analyzed in the communication literature, you yourself should be able to apply the dimensions of those operationalizations to real, observed behaviors and events. So, since we know what engagement is and how it is measured, we should be able to look at specific campaign content and responses to that content to assess the extent to which that content engaged audiences. Lastly, case studies are methodologically flexible, so you do not have to have advanced knowledge of social scientific research methods to write a thought-provoking, insightful, and useful case study. They often employ a combination of critical and qualitative methods, and you have been introduced to qualitative methods for finding trends in qualitative data in this text.

If you decide to pursue a case study, here are some suggestions for how to go about it:

1. Choose a communication situation or event to apply the concepts from your literature review: a crisis, campaign, social movement, or other socially and/or historically important event. Chances are that you chose the topic you wrote your paper about because you wanted to *understand something*— how something works, why something happens—and a case study is an opportunity to apply those concepts to explore real world events.

2. Look over the conceptualizations and operationalizations in the literature you have reviewed. What theories and related concepts are most relevant to the case you are planning to study? Communication case studies are often grounded in a set of concepts related to a single theory or a set of clearly defined, interrelated concepts.

3. Describe the context and importance of the case being studied. Explain the events leading up to the event, and offer clear research questions that will guide your analysis that link your theory/concepts to the case being explored.

4. Look closely at the communication relevant to your case. Use the diverse search strategies covered in this book to search through broadcast and print news coverage, blogs, discussions, press releases, and social media to see the case from as many angles as possible. How did the media cover it? How did the people or organizations involved communicate? How did people respond? What was the outcome of the event?

5. Apply the theories and concepts from your literature review to evaluate, critique, and explain what happened in the specific case you are researching. Did things occur as the research suggests they should or would? Why or why not?

6. Reach conclusions about the event: What was done well versus not done well? Also use this as an opportunity to consider the theories and concepts you applied: Did you find what you would expect to find based on previous research? What are the implications of your findings for the theory and concepts you applied? Did your findings suggest that the concepts are reliable and valid or not? What are the limitations of your application?

7. Write a narrative of the case. Case studies are typically written in the form of a narrative, beginning with the historical background of the case, then going into the concepts being applied, how the communications being analyzed were found and selected, then systematically analyzing the communications to reach conclusions about the event.

8. Share your findings through conference presentations, publication, or online publishing.

B. Professional Uses of Writing and Presenting Skills

Being successful after graduation is about both the knowledge you have and your ability to acquire new knowledge and skills as things change. It's great to know *how* to tweet via Twitter. It's more valuable to know *why* Twitter—and other social networks—are popular and how people use them. These are questions that are answered through careful research, and you now have the tools to access, interpret, and apply that research. So, as things change (and they will change dramatically over your lifetime) you will have the skills to acquire new knowledge and adapt to those changes and also to communicate to others through writing about and presenting ideas so you can share your knowledge. Clearly, this has professional benefits. There are also careers that specifically apply research skills.

Clearly, no one textbook and no one class can teach you everything you need to know to pursue a particular career. But the skills developed in classes that teach academic writing and research do have practical professional value for numerous careers in media, professional communications, and business. Here we highlight two such careers: blogging and editing.

1. Using Research Skills as a Blogger

Professional blogging can be used to generate income, promote a business, and as a job, if you have blog content and solid writing that will attract readers. The Bureau of Labor Statistics (BLS) (2012) pointed out that: "As professional writers, bloggers must be excellent communicators and need to understand what content most appeals to their audiences. Bloggers also have to be disciplined to produce high-quality research and writing, while trying to meet deadlines or to post breaking news" (p. 16).

Much like TV content or radio, the number of readers a blog has affects the advertising revenue that the blog generates. For information on making money as a blogger, read this brief, informative article from *US News & World Report:* http://money. usnews.com/money/articles/2009/05/19/how-to-earn-money-as-a-professional-blogger.

US News & World Report article

Many corporations also hire professional bloggers to maintain customer relationships, provide product and service information, etc. For example, check out http://jobs.problogger.net for information about current professional blogging opportunities. If you end up owning your own business, creating and maintaining a blog that supports your products with well-written content and solid evidence can be a great, free promotional tool.

Jobs available for bloggers

Some features of blogs fit well with the projects and skills we've worked on in this book. For example, Inc.com offers pointers on the elements of successful blogs: Establish your expertise, update when you have something new and interesting to say, interact with readers and read their feedback, and use online tools to promote your blog (i.e., Facebook and Twitter). The skills covered in this text can help you develop a blog in several ways:

- We have developed the ability to find and evaluate diverse types of information for use in your posts. You can now find evidence to support your claims from reliable, credible, and relevant sources. Offering solid evidence in support of product claims increases the persuasiveness of your content.
- The ability to find trends and themes in information and offer a reasoned critique in blog posts can help you present well-reasoned arguments and refute or rebut arguments or claims that may injure the product or idea you are promoting.
- Distilling information down and presenting clear and organized explanations of complex ideas is essential, as brief explanations of complex information are preferable in online formats.
- Focused writing is also essential online, which goes hand-in-hand with distilling information down. Blog posts should be focused on both the niche filled by the blog and the topic being discussed.
- Citing information to establish expertise and make valid, reasoned arguments is also valuable online. In blogs this is often done using hyperlinks to the content being referenced rather than formal APA citations, though some blog posts do also include a reference list.

2. Using Research Skills for Fact Checking and Copy Editing

Beyond blogging for personal and professional reasons, there are also careers in writing and editing that apply the skills taught in this book, such as fact checking and copy editing. The Education Portal explains that fact checking involves delving "deeply into stated facts and information to improve the quality of written materials" (para. 2). This type of career requires "Internet research and analytic skills, attention to detail and quality reading comprehension skills… [a]ccuracy and diligence" (para. 2).

Copy editing is one career option that combines skills in fact checking and writing. Traditionally, these types of careers were available with newspaper, book, and magazine publishers, but they are increasingly freelance positions and may include copy editing print or online content. The BLS' (2014) *Occupational Outlook Handbook* offers the following description of copy editing careers:

> **Copy editors** review copy for errors in grammar, punctuation, and spelling and check the copy for readability, style, and agreement with editorial policy. They suggest revisions… may carry out research, confirm sources for writers, and verify facts, dates, and statistics (para. 4).

The skills involved in writing your first literature review, including finding facts, evaluating sources, and editing are great first steps toward careers in professional writing and editing. If you have found this process interesting, you may want to pursue courses in technical writing, editing, and journalism.

C. Present Your Research in a Professional and/or Academic Portfolio

Even if you don't see professional writing in your future, the writing projects you complete as a student are excellent artifacts to include in a professional portfolio, particularly after you have received feedback from your instructors and edited your work. We encourage our students to keep their work throughout their undergraduate careers and use this work to build a portfolio that demonstrates professional skills.

One of the key strategies to finding a job in media and communication is having an online professional portfolio (Culver & Seguin, 2014). As a new college graduate, you will rely heavily on your coursework when developing your resume and marketing yourself to prospective employers. Specifically, your resume and cover letter should discuss *courses and projects* completed that demonstrate the development of *concrete skills*. Anyone can say they are a "good communicator." However, communication majors should be able to point to campaigns they have designed, groups they have worked in, research they have conducted, and presentations that they have given that demonstrate specific communication skills in interpersonal, group, public, and written communication.

Similarly, if you are applying to graduate school, it is helpful to take this same approach to your graduate school applications. Develop a resume and provide a writing sample that highlights your writing and researching skills, such as the literature review you just completed.

The easiest and least obtrusive way to present a portfolio of your college work—whether you are looking for a career or going on for graduate or professional education—is by creating professional social network profiles *and* a website. That way, you can simply include the web address for your portfolio in your resume rather than trying to mail a portfolio or lug a portfolio to an interview. Also, online portfolios can easily be submitted as a link in a cover letter or resume, even when a writing sample is not explicitly requested. When employers or graduate programs do ask for a writing sample, submit it in the format they requested, though you can also include the link to your portfolio so they can explore other works you have created.

Your literature review, case studies, and other projects you have completed over the course of your college career can be arranged in an online portfolio to serve as evidence of the skills you claim in your resume. Here are a few guidelines for putting together an online portfolio (Smith, 2013):

- **Have a headline** for the portfolio that 1) is likely to be picked up in online searches and 2) reflects the focus, or purpose, of your website.
- **Write an "about me" section** for the portfolio that serves many of the same functions of a cover letter: introduces you as a prospective employee, points out highlights from your resume, and previews the artifacts in your portfolio. This is essentially a "welcome page" for the website.
- **Include contact information.** At the very least, provide an (appropriate) email address that employers and others can use to contact you. Consider having a professional email alias explicitly for resumes, portfolios, and job application websites.
- **Write a resume** that overviews your coursework and professional development and highlights skills and accomplishments associated with both. The unique benefits of an online portfolio compared to a traditional one- or two-page uploaded or emailed resume are that you can use hyperlinks, multimedia, and formatting to make the resume interactive, more developed, and truly showcase your skills. In addition to communicating more about you as a candidate, an online interactive resume also speaks to your technical skills as a prospective employee. Because of the medium differences, there are some unique guidelines for developing interactive, online resumes:
    - When posting your resume online, do not include your personal address.
    - Collect videos, audio recordings, hyperlinks to websites or blogs, pdfs of brochures, advertisements, and papers you have created for your courses; also include letters of recommendation, awards, etc. to serve as evidence of your specific skills.
    - It is best to save these items as pdf files to ensure that formatting stays consistent for viewers who may be using different types of devices to look at your page.
    - Link directly to relevant portfolio elements from the resume, but for ease of use be sure that they open in a new window so that browsers can easily exit out of any linked content and be back at your resume.

- **Use organization and navigation to organize the elements of your website**. In addition to the hyperlinks in your resume, it is helpful to present information in separate pages throughout your resume. The website should be easy to navigate, with pages that contain similar or related content and some kind of explanation of that content. Think about how you read websites and navigate their content. You probably use the "Home" button to get back when you have been following hyperlinks; it's always helpful to have links to the main pages of the website organized in tabs along the top or left side of the page on each page within the website.
  - Group together related portfolio content. For example, have your complete resume on one page, have another page that features your writing, and another that features your awards, etc.
  - On every page, always have a "home" link that takes people back to the home page. It is also helpful to have website navigation on each page so people can easily go from one page to another then another within your website without having to go to the homepage each time.
  - The writing, formatting, and color scheme should be professional, clean, and easy to read throughout the site, and should also be consistent. Using existing themes and templates can help with this.

- **Proof it and test it**. Have several different people access your site, check all of the links, and read through the content. Ask them for brutally honest feedback. Also, most colleges and universities have a career services center. They may be able to help you develop, organize, and proof your website content.

There are many options available for creating and maintaining a portfolio of your work online, we will review just a few options: Social networks, portfolio-building websites, and websites/blogs.

1. Social Networks

LinkedIn allows you to upload documents, such as pdfs of completed projects, throughout your profile. You can also put detailed information in your profile about your education, work history, and skills. The unique feature of LinkedIn is that you link to people you know and develop a professional network. You can see the people in your connections' networks as well, so it is a great way to develop a professional portfolio and to share that with a network of professionals, including your peers, professors, coworkers, and former employers. People can post recommendations to your profile, and also endorse you for certain skills relevant to your experience. Therefore, it serves as a portfolio including a resume, method of creating and maintaining professional contacts, and evidence of professional endorsements.

You can learn more about LinkedIn here: www.linkedin.com and check out Dr. Curnalia (www.linkedin.com/pub/rebecca-curnalia/4b/74/504) and Dr. Ferris' (www.Linkedin.com/in/amberferris/) LinkedIn profiles.

LinkedIn

Dr. Curnalia's
LinkedIn Profile

Dr. Ferris' LinkedIn
Profile

2. Portfolio-Building Websites

Strikingly is an example of a portfolio-building website. It has a series of templates that you can choose from to develop your website, and those templates include different pages that you can quickly "plug content into." You can explore this website by visiting http://www.strikingly.com/s/discover.

Strikingly
portfolios

3. Websites

Blogging websites, such as **WordPress** or **Blogger,** or Website software such as **Google Sites**, can be used to create a website where you upload and update your portfolio. These websites offer more flexibility than LinkedIn (which has prescribed content areas), but use of blogs and personal websites require that you build your own audience.

Some of the advantages of WordPress are that there are clear, professional templates to choose from; there is the option to create as many pages as you would like; and you may organize pages however you feel is best. That being said, though you have much more flexibility in terms of the types and layout of content on WordPress, this also means that you should apply the principles of good website design when putting your portfolio together. You can see Dr. Curnalia's Wordpress page here: http://drcurnalia.wordpress.com/about/.

Dr. Curnalia's
WordPress

D. Concluding Thoughts

Whether you pursue a career in academics by going on to graduate school, work in professional writing and editing, or pursue another career in communication, we hope we have given you a solid set of skills that will help you as a lifelong learner and writer in our text-driven, information-saturated world. In the introduction to this text, we discussed information literacy, critical thinking, problem solving, and writing as the skills our graduates need to make important life decisions and to be professionally successful. Though some of what we teach in this text is specific to academic research, such as using APA style, much of what we have covered is relevant to professional communication in general: having a clear focus to your writing, finding and using the best available sources, paying attention to details when reading source content, identifying trends in content, organizing evidence to support conclusions, practicing quality writing and careful editing, and presenting findings via different channels to reach different audiences.

REFERENCES

Bureau of Labor Statistics (2012). Bloggers and webcomic artists: Careers in online creativity. *Occupational Outlook Quarterly*. Retrieved from http://www.bls.gov/opub/ooq/2012/fall/art02.pdf

Bureau of Labor Statistics (2014). What editors do. *Occupational Outlook Handbook*. Retrieved from http://www.bls.gov/ooh/media-and-communication/editors.htm#tab-2

Culver, S. H., & Seguin, J. (2014). *Media career guide: Preparing for jobs in the 21st Century* (9th ed.). Boston: Bedford St. Martin's.

Education Portal (n.d.). Become a fact checker: Education and career path. Retrieved from http://education-portal.com/articles/Become_a_Fact_Checker_Education_and_Career_Roadmap.html

Inc.com. (n.d.). 8 tips for successful social bloggers. Retrieved from http://www.inc.com/ss/8-tips-for-effective-social-blogging

Smith, J. (2013). Why every job seeker should have a personal website, and what it should include. *Forbes*. Retrieved online from http://www.forbes.com/sites/jacquelynsmith/2013/04/26/why-every-job-seeker-should-have-a-personal-website-and-what-it-should-include/

ACTIVITIES

1. Find a real-world situation that your literature review relates to from the news, entertainment media, or your own personal experiences. Use the case study guidelines in this chapter to write a brief application of the concepts from your paper to explain and critique that real-world event.

2. Build a LinkedIn profile or WordPress website that includes a resume and also features your projects and accomplishments in Communication courses. Include PDFs of awards, letters of recommendation or recognition, your research papers, and links to your YouTube presentations.